PRAISE FOR

# PARIS BLUE

"Not every true story is like a good novel, but this one is. Not every memoir of first love has a satisfying ending, but this one does. The confluence of first love with becoming an artist makes this memoir special."

—John Irving, best-selling author of seventeen novels

"Julie Scolnik's memoir, *Paris Blue,* brings full spectrum color to a love affair with Paris, music, and a man whose limited vision couldn't keep her from shining. Filled with sensuousness, sound, and light, as well as the hard edge of truth, this story of first love grips the reader tight."

—Jennifer Rosner, author of *If a Tree Falls* and *The Yellow Bird Sings*

"The haunting impact of our first true and deep love stays with us the remainder of our lives, and all of us struggle in some way to put those emotions—the exultation, the revelries of passion and belonging, and the ultimate scars of loss—into a workable context. This memoir explores the process, including the barriers, the relapses and the ultimate conclusion that one's life needs to find its own forms."

—Greg Fields, author of *Arc of the Comet* and *Through the Waters and the Wild*

"*Paris Blue*, Julie Scolnik's memoir of first love in Paris, is written with the tender romanticism of Wordsworth and the devastating realism of Flaubert. Her lyrical writing about music transforms these discordant halves into a compelling whole, creating a dazzling love letter to a life lived in music."

—**Linda Katherine Cutting, author of** *Memory Slips*

"Captivating! *Paris Blue* could speak to anyone who's ever yearned for closure that never came. But Julie Scolnik's memoir doesn't simply try to make sense of a bewildering romance; through telling the story she manages to bless the past, in all its complexity, while giving herself fully to the present."

—**Leah Hager Cohen, author of** *Strangers and Cousins* **and** *The Grief of Others*

"Julie Scolnik's beautiful page turner of a memoir captures with rare insight the power of music, words, and Paris to drive love to madness. To read her pitch perfect writing is to relive the exhilarations and vulnerabilities of one's twenties."

—**Judith Coffin, author of** *Sex, Love, and Letters: Writing Simone de Beauvoir*

"Nothing burns hotter than young love, and Julie Scolnik captures that singular fervor in *Paris Blue*. But her memoir is more than that: it's a deeply felt, bittersweet reflection on how youthful passion changes you and clings to you, forever."

—**Howard Reich, author of** *Prisoner of Her Past*, **and** *The Art of Inventing Hope: Intimate Conversations with Elie Wiesel*

"*Paris Blue* drew me in from the opening descriptions of France through a young American woman's eyes, and its textural details match the depth of the story: a tale of love and exploration. The letters that begin each chapter evoke deep romance and allow the reader to share the author's sense of possibility. In the final chapters, time moves more quickly, and Scolnik's growing sense of discovery brings wonderful closure to the story."

—**Alex Myers, author of** *Revolutionary* **and** *Continental Divide*

"Who hasn't dreamed of living a year in Paris? Scolnik lived that dream when she was 20, and brings us inside the exhilaration and heartaches of first love, observing her relationship with Luc in such rich detail that she makes it both unique and universal."

—**Michael Blanding, author of** *North by Shakespeare* **and**
*The Map Thief*

*Paris Blue*

by Julie Scolnik

ISBN 978-1-64663-469-9

Cover art by Marcelo Lavallén

Published by

 köehlerbooks™

3705 Shore Drive
Virginia Beach, VA 23455
800-435-4811
www.koehlerbooks.com

A MEMOIR OF FIRST LOVE

# Paris Blue

## JULIE SCOLNIK

VIRGINIA BEACH
CAPE CHARLES

Part One

# ONE

———— ✦✦✦ ————

*Paris. June 1977*

*Dear Julie,*

*This letter won't reach you for days. When it does, I hope that you will have regained your equilibrium. As for me, I am sinking like a ship in a storm. Yesterday after you left, I lived through one of the most difficult days of my life. My body was knotted, as if, at 1:30, when your plane took off, all the existential anguish that you knew how to appease, surprised me again with more force, more tenacity.*

*Paris seems absurd. Yesterday, so as not to struggle against invincible forces, I drove down both rue Brown-Séquard and rue Bonaparte, willing you to appear. Please send me as much as you can about your life back home. You know where I work and live. But I can only try to imagine you in this vast unknown, and it's unbearable.*

*Luc*

❧

**PARIS. SEPTEMBER 1976—EIGHT MONTHS EARLIER.**

Perched on my toes, I peered over the upright piano and frowned at the fat gold Buddha wedged behind it. My elbow had inadvertently sent it flying while I was unpacking my music and I'd watched its rotund belly sail across the smooth dark wood and disappear with a thud. I wondered if Madame Cammas would even notice it was missing, and considered leaving it there until I left Paris the following June. It wasn't mine, after all, and I was scheming to decorate my room as I always had since I was ten years old—with pretty things that reminded me of home. Like my twelve Japanese rice paper woodcuts of the calendar months that had migrated from summer music camps to all my dorm rooms at Exeter and Wesleyan, each time animating an entire wall with vibrant color and whimsy. It would only be a matter of time before a cluster of rainbow-colored origami cranes would hover delicately over my bed. But the unexpected discovery of a piano in my own bedroom—even an old out-of-tune upright with antique yellow keys—convinced me that finding this lodging was fortuitous.

A few months earlier, when I was tracking down a room to rent in Paris for my junior year abroad, I was connected through my French Exeter roommate to a museum curator who rented a room each year to a student. A curator! I imagined she'd live in a grandiose limestone building built during the Belle Époque, her apartment filled with records, books, and paintings. What would I wear when she invited me to the opera?

But the day I arrived in Paris, my taxi turned instead onto a tiny, quiet street in the fifteenth *arrondissement* and stopped in front of 9, rue Brown-Séquard. Not one of the majestic Haussmann buildings I had read about, but charming nonetheless, with a very respectable entrance and characteristic black ironwork balustrades defining the upper floor windows.

I had slid out crisp new francs to pay the taxi driver—bills featuring stunning, colored portraits of Debussy, Berlioz, Cézanne, and Saint-Exupéry—even the money in France was artistic! I hobbled toward the entrance with my heavy bags and rang an oversized black bell. A dour *guardienne,* who bore an uncanny resemblance to the housekeeper in *Rebecca,* appeared and grimly indicated Madame Cammas' ground-floor apartment just inside the foyer to the right. I knocked twice before a stooped, boulder-bosomed elderly lady opened the door. Her wide mouth was turned up in a clownish smile, and layers of thin, crinkly skin draped her eyes. A mass of gray hair was pinned randomly on her head, and a shapeless print dress hung low to her lumpy calves.

"Bonjour Madame Cammas, I am Julie Scolnik," I said in perfect schoolgirl French. "I hope this isn't too early for you." It was eight o'clock.

"*MAIS NON!*" The old lady's voice was thunderous and unevenly timbered, vaulting from chest voice to falsetto within the same word.

"*ENTREZ! ENTREZ!*" She tried unsuccessfully to pick up my unwieldy suitcase, but managed instead to drag my smaller leather satchel through the entryway without lifting it off the ground. Flustered, she led me down the hallway.

"THIS IS YOUR ROOM!" she bellowed in French, indicating the high-ceilinged bedroom at the end of the hall.

I glanced at the piano, fireplace, and armoire. "It's perfect. I love it," I said.

"*TANT MIEUX!* All the better!" Madame answered loudly enough for the people upstairs to hear.

My landlady scurried like a muskrat into an antiquated kitchen, opening the door of her waist-high fridge.

"You can use this shelf for your groceries," she announced as she pointed to a small empty shelf above one crammed full of tiny yogurts, leftover soups, and plastic-wrapped, fatty, mystery meat.

"When you make a phone call, you put one franc in this black box!" Madame warbled, after leading me into a large somber living room, furnished with dark furniture and an old television in the corner. It was decidedly devoid of books, records, or paintings. *She can't be the curator at a museum,* I thought. *Maybe she sells the postcards.*

"And for ten francs extra a month you can take a bath three times a week," she added. "Hang your dresses in this armoire in the hall, with mine. You'll need to buy your own sheets, but you can borrow some from me until you do."

I tuned in and out as Madame Cammas recited other house rules in a very loud French falsetto. The scratchy sore throat that had incubated on the red eye from Boston was beginning to throb with pain and I desperately wanted to shut my eyes. But I accepted my landlady's offer to tour my new neighborhood, so out we went, past the local post office, bank, and small *épicerie.* We stopped at the closest metro stop, Gare Montparnasse, to buy my *carte orange,* the laminated monthly metro and bus pass to anywhere in Paris. On the way home, a blast of warm air shot up from the subway vents and caught us off guard. We both struggled to keep the world from seeing our bare legs—a hunched, shapeless octogenarian, grinning and embarrassed by the sudden exposure of her vein-mapped calves, and a culture-shocked American college girl in suede clogs and batik wrap-around skirt.

Back in my room, I unpacked my large suitcase, then unlatched the armoire where I placed my clothes in small, folded piles. Tall French windows with shutters looked out onto the quiet street. *Here they just call them windows,* I thought. I would repeat this to myself quite often, with French bread, French fries, and French braids.

When all my music and belongings had been put away (ignoring the Buddha behind the piano), I leaned into the spotted mirror over the mantel to inspect my agonizing throat and realized, in my miserable state, that nobody was going to take care of me. There would be no one bringing me aspirin in the middle of the night as my mother did when I was a little girl, no warm, soothing broth brought to me by my father. I longed to postpone being an adult for a day or two, just until it didn't feel as if a knife were slicing through my throat every time I swallowed, just until the inevitable onset of a horrendous cold had passed. I wasn't savvy and independent like some of the girls at Exeter and Wesleyan who had been riding the New York subway system alone since they were nine. I had never lived in any big city before; I only knew the tame, rolling green campuses of my schools in New Hampshire and Connecticut.

I went through three boxes of French tissues during my first few days in the City of Light, sneezing violently and blowing my nose till it was red and sore. With watery eyes, I stuffed tissues into my pockets and found my way to Galeries Lafayette, the Macy's of France, to buy sheets and a small radio. Days later when I finally began to recover, I flung my shutters wide open, skipped out of my room, and wandered down to Montparnasse, stopping at a dazzling flower market for two dozen lavender roses. Then all at once, the stunning reality began to sink in: I was twenty years old and living in Paris.

# TWO

Dear Julie,

This past weekend I went to the countryside in Anjou. It was sumptuous and magnificent and full of scents. In a beautiful country house, I allowed time to pass, thinking about you, about these months together, while listening to Schubert, interspersed with sounds of nature.

And now I am back in Paris which is too full of memories: the flowers you threw into the Seine on our last day together on June 26, The Red Lion Café, St. Germain, Bus #48. I want you to know how at every moment my life here is hard for me without you. I try to stop thinking about you so that I can work, eat, and sleep, but you always return to me full force by a ridiculous little detail.

One week ago, we went to Versailles. And yesterday, I relived, hour by hour, our separation. I'll write more tomorrow. Tonight, I'll just listen to music. The flute will obsess me to my core.

Luc

Being on my own in a city as intrinsically poetic as Paris proved a heady mix for a small-town Maine girl like myself. At first, I floated through the streets during the calm morning hours in a blurry state of disbelief, light-headed from bus fumes that mingled with the intoxicating aroma of warm croissants wafting from the *boulangeries*.

*"Gather ye rosebuds while ye may,"* so the poem says.

Two years into an undergraduate degree in a bland Connecticut town, I longed to gather mine. And why not in Europe, which I had craved ever since spending a few weeks in the South of France at nineteen, playing in the masterclasses of world-famous flutists. Now I was to study privately in Paris with one of my teachers from that summer.

Each day I strolled down the wide airy sidewalks of Boulevard du Montparnasse to reach my classes on a small side street, rue de Chevreuse. Morning was my favorite time to sit in the grand cafés, with early golden light slanting across my round, marble table. It wasn't long before I felt like a regular at Le Dôme and La Rotonde, two of the iconic ones along the way.

My confidence grew with my daily routines, as I sauntered each morning over to my habitual corner and ordered a big *café au lait*. It always arrived with two paper-wrapped sugar cubes, tiny luxuries next to the pedestrian packets of loose sugar served in the U.S. Even though I never took sugar in my coffee, the minuscule etchings of Parisian churches and calligraphic letters on them enticed me to reach for one now and then. I couldn't help thinking about and imitating my Russian immigrant grandfather, whom I had watched countless times bite off half a sugar cube, hold it in front of his mouth, and take sip after sip of coffee through it, until it had completely dissolved on his tongue.

Exuding self-importance in these cafés was crucial if I wanted to command respect in the subtle power struggle with the waiters. I knew that the slim, black-vested servers weaving gracefully between tables could ignore me endlessly if they deemed me unworthy of their attention. So I prudently ordered in a manner that wouldn't peg me as an American. Never a *café au lait* but a *grand crème,* never an *espresso* but a *petit noir.* If I ordered my coffee that way, there would be no odd look in the waiter's face that registered *une étrangère* (a foreigner), no split second of hesitation before hearing, "*Très bien, mademoiselle, tout de suite.*"

When I stopped in one of the cafés after class in the late afternoon, it was brimming with regular patrons. I began to recognize certain types— elderly French ladies sitting shoulder to shoulder looking out onto the street, their miniature terriers perched on chairs beside them; businessmen in suits nursing tall beers; students smoking cigarettes and writing notes at their espresso-cluttered tables; graying, long-haired intellectuals with scarves, looking important, retired, and committed to café life as a means of keeping the old political discussions alive over their *plats du jour.*

I walked for hours, sometimes entire days, until my calves ached and my feet pulsed with pain. The breathtaking splendor around me created a bottomless pit of yearning that made it impossible to choose in which direction to wander—along the *quais* past the dark green kiosks of old books, prints, and maps, the Seine glittery from the early morning sun; or down the cobbled streets of the Latin quarter, past picturesque squares and fountains like Place de la Contrescarpe. I couldn't get over the intense thrill of instantly becoming part of any Paris scene I chose, as if I had just waltzed into a French film or painting. For the first three months I had only one thought: why would anyone live anywhere else if they could live in Paris?

Lured to the countless window displays of ravishing fruit tarts, their symmetrical spirals of strawberries, apricots, or figs glistening with glazes, I had quests each week for the quintessential version of my alternating favorite pastries. First it was the plump, cream-filled *éclair au café* with its amber strip of sweet coffee icing on top, then the sumptuous, caramelized round apple chunks sitting atop flaky pastry in the *Tarte Tatin.*

"A quarter of a baguette, please, not too dark," I would ask at a bakery each day when it was time to think about dinner. And then I would stop by a small neighborhood market to buy an oversized plastic bottle of Evian water, a tiny glass yogurt, a small piece of Morbier or Gruyère cheese, a tomato, a bag of carrots and assorted fruit. I would return to my room to picnic cross-legged on my bed while I listened to my radio and read assignments for school. I never ventured into Madame Cammas' decrepit kitchen to cook.

I spoke freely with dozens of strangers—women in markets, men in cafés, waiters, policemen. Speaking a foreign language made all my conversations feel make-believe, as if I could say anything and not be held accountable. Intentionally using *tu*, the familiar form of "you," with everyone—young or elderly, bureaucrat or schoolboy—I knew I could get away with it, and enjoyed the perverse pleasure of disarming people with this faux pas.

"What are you doing in Paris?" people would ask in my daily encounters.

"Oh, I'm studying the flute with Olivier Lefevre," I would answer, delighted with their reactions, "and taking courses in literature and *philo* near Montparnasse."

"Oh, you're not French?" they would continue, this time with a smile, when they heard what they called a trace of an accent.

"*Vous êtes Italienne?*"

"*Non, non, Américaine!*" I'd correct them, and then wait for them to invariably praise my French, which I would deny with false modesty.

I knew I had a good accent, ever since my sixth grade French classes, when I first discovered the palpable sensuality of forming French words with my lips and tongue. I would practice the phrases in class under my breath, waiting to deliver them flawlessly when my turn came to speak.

The Wesleyan Program in Paris held its classes in a sweet, intimate, white brick building called Reid Hall, owned and administered by Columbia University. It had a small reference library, a flowering central courtyard, and classrooms with large round tables. Several American universities took part in this program of literature, philosophy, film, and other French civilization courses. The professors were drawn from various highbrow Paris universities like the Sorbonne and Sciences Po, and over the years had boasted a faculty of distinguished well-known scholars such as Roland Barthes, Nathalie Sarraute, and Alain Robbe-Grillet.

A few of my teachers lectured us pedantically in booming voices even though we were only ten around a table. They exuded arrogance and condescension, as if they had accepted this job reluctantly, undoubtedly believing American students to be frivolous and unworthy of their time. To terrorize us right away, one of them assigned Stendhal's entire seven-hundred-page *Le Rouge et le Noir* to read in just a few days. I looked forward to my classes, the only drawback being that they were with other American students, never the way to immerse oneself in a foreign language. Each class only met once or twice a week, however, allowing me plenty of time to read the novels and practice for my flute lessons.

It might have seemed a bit of an odd decision for a serious music student like myself to be enrolled in an academic program rather than the highly esteemed Paris Conservatory. But when I first conceived the plan, it seemed perfect: I would register for Wesleyan's Program in Paris and receive full academic credit while fulfilling a long-standing desire to study with Olivier Lefevre. I had met the well-known flutist when I took part in his masterclasses during a summer festival in Nice, France, just after my freshman year of college. But something transpired that summer that shook my resolve that he was the mentor I needed.

Of all the teachers I played for during the festival, including the very famous Jean-Pierre Rampal, it was Lefevre's playing and teaching that most inspired me. It was a bit of an exotic dream at first. The conservatory was perched in the ancient part of Nice called Cimiez, far up winding, cobbled streets teeming with tropical vegetation. The tall, open, French windows of the gold-domed music studios looked out onto the distant clay-tiled roofs and quaint ports of the turquoise Mediterranean Sea. I had made a plan to share a room in a boarding house with my roommate from Exeter, Myriam, who had come to study violin.

Though I had just turned nineteen and Lefevre was twice my age, it seemed I struck his fancy. This was new to me. I had only recently become a confident college girl—thinner and more comfortable in my body, which I revealed happily in halter sundresses and leggy skirts—and Lefevre noticed. He called me "*La Belle de Nice*" when I walked into class, and would take my arm, pretending to lead me back out the door. "See you all later!" he would say to the others. He also pegged me right away as one of the best players in the class and gave me attention I'd never had before.

"And when you *breave,* you must keep *zee* life! It is *passion* and anguish you must show in your playing," as he grabbed my shoulders in a lustful gesture.

"Yes, I understand," I answered.

"But *of course* you do!" he said, eliciting laughter from the audience. "Your sound is a dream but only now are you learning to use it, to play like a woman." I knew this was cheap romance novel drivel. But the attention was compelling, and I was smitten.

On the last day of the Lefevre masterclasses, I performed the formidable Reinecke Sonata in the morning, and celebrated by going to the beach with Myriam in the afternoon, dropping in to listen to the final five o'clock class on my way home. My bathing suit straps were visible under my sundress, and my hair and skin were sun-drenched from my daily swims in the warm, salty, Mediterranean Sea. When the class was over at 7 o'clock, Lefevre came over to me, put his arm around my shoulder, and made no effort to hide his low gaze. He made some comments in French about me to some boys nearby, but I caught none of it.

"You've come from the beach? Shall we go have another swim?" he asked. "It's still so beautiful out, and I really need the change after so many hours of teaching inside."

This put me in a cruelly awkward position. I loathed setting myself apart from the others—there was nothing more abhorrent than seeing one student going off with the teacher. But I was so out of my element, both flattered and ill-equipped to know how to respond. So down the curved marble staircase of the conservatory we went, together. Outside, I got into his red convertible in the circular driveway, writhing with embarrassment as I closed the door. I wanted to wear a sign on my back that said, "This is not what it looks like."

We drove down Boulevard de Cimiez towards the sea. He parked his car in the port of Cap Ferrat, and he led the way to a secluded nook on the cliffs that he no doubt frequented quite often. We jumped into the ocean, bobbed in the waves together, and came up on the rocks to rest. The low sun sequined the azure waves.

"You must be young," he said, with an intense scrutiny that made me squirm. "Twenty years old?"

"Nineteen," I answered.

"Like a piece of fruit," he added, touching the peach fuzz of my bronzed upper arm.

"I want to *take* you on those rocks," he added playfully. I didn't understand what he said at the time. The French word he used was *violer*.

"You know, you have only one earring," he smiled at me.

"Oh, it must have come off in the ocean," I uttered sheepishly as I removed the other cheap silver hoop and flung it over the cliffs into the water. A moment later I stood up to discover that I'd been sitting on the first one. I laughed with embarrassment and tossed that one into the ocean, too.

"I *lof* your face! It's so *espresseeve!*" he said in English.

We drove into a neighboring net-webbed port. After we were seated at a candlelit table on a restaurant terrace, Lefevre ordered a platter of teeny fried fish, deep bowls of bouillabaisse, and a carafe of wine. I had never felt so worldly.

"I take things seriously," I tried in my tentative French as we left the restaurant and walked to his car, after he implied all evening what was on his mind—going "*chez moi.*"

"Besides, I have a roommate," I added, when I saw that he wasn't listening.

"You are *adorable!*" he laughed, as he headed his Renault up toward the old section of the city. "Wouldn't she be at the outdoor concert at the monastery with all of the other music students?" he asked as we arrived at my rundown villa behind Hotel Cimiez.

My silence told him that he was right. I didn't want him to come back to my room, but I had no idea how to refuse. Reaching for the key on our habitual ledge above the door, I breathed a sigh of relief that Myriam had forgotten to leave it there. Undeterred, Lefevre led me by the hand through the clematis-covered black iron gate to the dark garden in the back. Leaning me up against the cold stone wall, he began to kiss me mechanically as his hand lifted my sundress and found its way into my panties.

"I'm not protected," I whispered in French.

"Don't worry," he answered, "I'll be careful." He began fidgeting with the button on his pants. I felt like stone, paralyzed, as in a dream when you cannot scream.

In a moment he had lifted my left thigh and was inside me. He thrust for twenty seconds, then withdrew and ejaculated silently in the bushes with an oddly blank look on his face. He zipped his pants and walked me to the front of the villa.

"Are you going to be all right?" he asked as he got into his convertible and drove off.

Without the key to my room, I was stranded for an hour in the dark as I waited for Myriam to return from the concert.

Lefevre had invited me to accompany him to Saint Paul de Vence for a concert, and I found myself counting on that time to give more meaning to the garden incident. However, during a final celebratory dinner with all the flute students the next night, Lefevre casually announced that he couldn't make that trip with me after all. And then it hit me. I felt foolish and demeaned, and cried silently in my pillow for the next week.

The meaningless-yet-sordid physical encounter should have shamed him more than it did me. Going forward, I was free to use him for what mattered most to me—my music. Even before this incident occurred, he had told me to come study with him in Paris, and implied that he could get me started with some freelance work, further complicating the choice for me.

Though the memory still haunted me when I arrived in Paris for the school year, fifteen months had passed, and I believed Lefevre's reputation as a teacher outweighed my embarrassing personal history with him. I didn't want to derail my meticulous plans. The first time I saw Lefevre for a lesson in Paris, he tried to erase the incident in Nice with a simple acknowledgement that it "wasn't *l'amour*," and asked me if I "held it against him." He invited me several more times to meet him at one of his rehearsals or recording sessions in Paris. I finally realized that I needed to convey a new aloofness to avoid any further misunderstandings. I fancied myself a serious musician as I walked with my black flute case tucked under my arm to my weekly lessons near the Duroc metro station.

CR

After a couple of weeks, I prided myself on mastering multiple combinations of buses and metros to transport me anywhere in the city.

I avoided anything that could mark me as a tourist, so I never waited in line to visit monuments or museums. In a city so rich with history, I knew very little of it. Even when I stood facing the breathtaking stained glass of Sainte-Chapelle, I never cared to read about the Biblical stories they depicted. The mosaics of blue beveled glass beneath the ancient, vaulted ceilings cast their spell each time I entered, but it was the visceral *feeling* of history in Paris which held me in awe.

The first time I walked into the Jeu de Paume, the museum housing all the Impressionists during this era, I nearly had to steady myself against a railing, so overwhelming was it to see those famous works of Renoir, Monet, and Degas in person. Even then, I spent little time at each painting, walking instead through the ornate salons the way one might stroll through the grounds of a formal Italian garden, letting the centuries pour over me in an intuitive, emotional way.

Before long, I had ditched my clunky Frye boots and faded denim skirt in exchange for tall, high-heeled brown leather boots and a thin beige trench coat. I felt pleased with my transformation as I glanced at my new reflection in store windows. But the modest boost in my self-image was quickly obliterated by chic French women with elongated strides who lived to intimidate and run me off the sidewalk. I could never quite master their sense of urgency about where they were going.

Once I bought a silk scarf at *Printemps*, and tried to tie it around my neck in one of the many ways I saw French women do it. But after a mere few minutes, I found it unbearably confining, yanked it off, and stuffed it into my bag. I was invisible to the haughty saleswomen in clothing stores, and ladies behind pharmacy counters squinted at me coldly when I walked in, scrutinizing my face, ready to propose numerous products for its flaws.

Frenchmen, on the other hand, were another story. From respectable businessmen on the Champs-Elysées to young turtlenecked professors in the Latin Quarter, they were far from indifferent. They made no effort to hide their penetrating gazes as I passed them on sidewalks or sat across from them in subways or cafés. I suspected it had to do with the open look on my face and the slower pace in which I walked. The really unsavory ones would either start to talk to me and ask me, in mid-stride, if I wanted to get a drink, or say, "What a nice day it is to take a walk, *ein, Mademoiselle?*" Only in Paris would a homeless man declare in a gravelly voice from his bottle-strewn corner of the sidewalk, "It is very pretty, your little dress, *Mademoiselle!*"

Sometimes in the evening I'd leave the solitude of my room and head to the bustle and energy of the Latin Quarter to peruse bookstores and listen to street musicians. I'd pass by vendors' carts of smoky, warm, praline almonds that dark African men were selling in teeny, brown paper bags, waiting to earn another franc and tease another American girl.

*"You speeeek Eeengleesh?"* They would always try to engage an easy target like myself. I may have replaced my denim skirt, but I was still spotted right away as a foreigner, even without opening my mouth. I would try to walk by more quickly now, as if unaffected by stares, remarks, or vulgarity. Turning onto Quai Saint-Michel, I'd cross the street to walk directly by the Seine, leaning over the waist-high granite walls to look down at the water. The lights of the Préfecture de Police and the Palais de Justice would reflect back like a mirror as darkness crept over the city.

One day in late September I decided to search for a music history class to audit. It would have made more sense to try the conservatory first, but I ventured instead into the fifth *arrondissement* to explore the legendary Sorbonne. I wasn't used to city schools, and expected that, like American Universities, there would be separate buildings for music, science, and Romance Languages all clearly mapped out. The Sorbonne, however, covered several blocks, with each imposing building indistinguishable from the next. I stopped multiple students on the street to ask for help, with no success. Someone finally pointed to a possible building, though it was still a bit of a guess.

Once inside, there were no administrative offices anywhere in sight, and there was definitely no music coming from the rooms. Twenty minutes later I was still walking down convoluted corridors and up more flights of stairs. Frustrated, tired, and bad-tempered, I was about to give up when I decided to walk down one more unmarked corridor to read a paper-cluttered bulletin board at the end of it. As I stood facing it, a three-inch

square piece of cardboard materialized at eye level. On it were these words
in childlike handwriting:

JULIE:

MARSHALL WHO SOLD YOU

THE RING IN MAINE IS IN PARIS

AND WOULD LIKE TO FIND YOU. ÇA VA?

04 37 82 46 84

I was stupefied. How was this possible? Could this be for me? I had
purchased an inexpensive agate ring on the coast of Maine during the
summer, and had chatted with the friendly jewelry-maker behind the
counter. I had mentioned (as I had to everyone) that I was off to Paris in a
few weeks to study music. Besides my first name, that's all he knew. I tried the
number, but it was out of service. Marshall would never know that I saw his
note, but stumbling across it in such a way humbled me in a way I couldn't
explain. I was struck by great invisible forces around me, and I would soon
realize that this was not to be my only incident of happenstance and fate.

# THREE

Dear Julie,

*Thank you for your long letter, which helps me imagine your life halfway across the globe. It's so frustrating to me that even the rhythms of my days and nights, and the feelings they provoke, are out of sync with yours. What could you be doing at this hour? I am going to bed now, whereas for you it is only five o'clock. You must be in the midst of full activity. Horrible. When these words reach you, I imagine that it is daytime and the sun is shining, and that you are with a group of friends. That you forget me.*

*To think that just a year ago you were arriving in Paris, looking for a chorus to sing in! Knowing that you arrived here in September, four months before I even met you, makes me want to scream. If only we could go back in time.*

*Luc*

By October, chestnuts and leaves curling into tawny shades of gold were collecting in piles near the curbs of the grand tree-lined boulevards around the city. I found it comforting to shuffle through the crunchy leaves, but they left me aching with nostalgia for my favorite season in New England. I inhaled their scent and filled my pockets with handfuls of useless mahogany-smooth chestnuts.

Parisians still filled every table at outdoor cafés and every pale green metal chair in the Jardin du Luxembourg, but as the weeks passed, they draped their shoulders with sweaters and shawls and lingered in the last dwindling rays of the autumn sun before it disappeared behind buildings.

Then, no sooner did the calendar page turn to November than the skies grew dark, and the sun stayed hidden behind thick, steel gray clouds. Paris in the winter was for connoisseurs of melancholy, and I wondered whether I should stay in my program for only one semester. Though I loved my new life in this evocative city, by mid-November I was roaming the misty *quais* feeling hollow and lost. Sometimes, after an aimless walk along the Seine, I would return to the warmth of my room, stand in front of the mirrored mantel, and stare at my sad face. I'd feel a familiar tingling in my nose, then watch with fascination as a glassy film would rise up and blur the brown spheres looking back. It was a frequent occurrence, a bodily function like any other. I was so used to how it felt that once I knew what was coming, there was a certain satisfying inevitability to it. I would watch the tears pool inside my lower lid and anticipate the moment when the first drop would overflow onto my cheek. I thought back to certain boys that I had already turned away in my young life. Would it be too late to reach back in time?

I needed to find a way to fill the void, to connect somehow, nourish my hunger. I thought that joining a chorus might do wonders for my morale. Ever since music camp at thirteen when I was surprised to discover a strong soprano voice, singing had become essential to my equilibrium and well-being. As much as being enrolled at a conservatory would have afforded me the camaraderie of other music students in both orchestra and chamber music, practicing the flute alone in my room was lonely and isolating. Searching for a chorus became my single-minded focus.

My French film teacher, Annie Goldmann, heard about my search, and told me about a chorus her brother sang in. I decided to simply show up at a rehearsal and inquire.

I walked nervously around the perimeter of Église Saint Sulpice, the clack of my high heeled boots ricocheting loudly in the night air as I searched for an open door under endless foreboding archways. I must have circled the church three times and was starting to sweat and prickle under my sweater, when I finally made a mortifying entrance into a large rehearsal room. It was filled with chorus members who seemed to step out of a Fellini film, some throwing their heads back and shrieking with laughter, others speaking and moving melodramatically. They hadn't yet begun to rehearse, so I asked someone to indicate the director. I approached a daunting old man, and asked if he had any more room for sopranos.

"Wait here!" he barked at me, then walked away, leaving me in the middle of the room by the piano, while dozens of people stared from afar. After an interminable amount of time, he still hadn't returned, and it was more than I could bear. My face and body ablaze with humiliation, I swiveled quickly and flew out of the room toward the exit, every person there witnessing my escape. I ran across the street, down the subway stairs to the train, and returned home to rue Brown-Séquard, my safe refuge. I didn't need to sing. This cringe-worthy incident might have been enough to shatter my desire to find a chorus, had my luck not turned around the following week.

On an unseasonably balmy Friday afternoon, after my Marxism class on Dialectic Thought, which always demanded herculean concentration and left me confused and spent, I decided not to go home. I didn't know where I was headed when I flagged down a bus on Boulevard du Montparnasse. In Paris, I never knew. Sometimes it was only when a bus appeared in the distance that an idea would emerge. *Surprise me*, I often thought. On this particular day, I took a bus to the river, and then decided to walk along the *quais* before settling on a beautiful little café called Le Voltaire. It faced the Seine and the sprawling south side of the Louvre. I sat down at a cozy table on the terrace, warmed by heat lamps that hung from inside the awnings, as a violet dusk descended over the city. I took out a paperback and felt content with my choice.

A man had just left the table next to me, with the French daily newspaper, *Le Monde,* folded under an empty beer glass. I had long given up buying this paper after a few hopeless attempts to slog through its small French print and photo-less pages. The *International Herald Tribune* was the only way to get readable news when needed. The waiter was just coming by to take my order when I happened to glance over at the abandoned paper. I picked it up out of curiosity, when a small square notice jumped out at me. Tearing off the bottom right corner, I held it with two hands, and stared at these words in disbelief:

> THE CHORUS OF THE ORCHESTRE DE PARIS
>
> DANIEL BARENBOIM, MUSIC DIRECTOR
>
> AUDITIONS—ALL PARTS—SALLE PLEYEL
>
> DECEMBER 1, 1976—TEL. 758.26.36

That such a chorus even existed was already an incredible discovery! But with the world-renowned conductor, Daniel Barenboim? There was no better choral opportunity in the entire world! I clumsily bolted down the spiral staircase to the basement café telephone, and called the number. The secretary was very kind and surprisingly easy to understand, rarely the case for me on the phone. She took my name, and told me where and when to arrive for the audition. I ran across the street to flag down a bus in the direction of my favorite music store, Durand Musique, at Place de la Madeleine, and arrived just before they closed. I left the store with a single aria, *Voi Che Sapete,*[1] from Mozart's *Marriage of Figaro,* and began to work on it at the piano as soon as I got home.

When the audition date arrived, I tucked the flimsy sheet music into my bag to protect it, and was on my way. I was dressed in what I considered my most grownup look—a camel skirt, white scoop neck sweater, tall brown boots, and my long hair clipped back in a half ponytail. The bus took me to the eighth *arrondissement,* where I walked several blocks to Salle Pleyel, on rue du Faubourg St. Honoré.

My throat was parched, so when I spotted a café across the street, I headed to the bar and ordered a *Perrier tranche.* I smashed the lemon slice at the bottom with the long spoon, and, though it stung my throat, gulped it down. Walking through the stage door, marked *Entrée Des Artistes,* I followed the signs to the audition. A receptionist led me to an elegantly appointed waiting room where I met other new candidates, and we waited in companionable silence for our names to be called one at a time. In a few minutes I was brought into what I assumed was the Salle Pleyel green room—an elegant salon with grand piano and signed photographs of famous musicians on its walls. The secretary introduced me to the choral director, Arthur Oldham, a hefty, white-bearded Englishman seated behind a table. I sang my Mozart aria with the pianist they provided, and when I was finished, Oldham smiled broadly and asked me questions in English, making me feel instantly at ease.

"Have you sung in many choirs?

"Yes, I have, at my schools and summer programs for many years."

"Were they good ones?"

"Yes, excellent!"

"How are you about getting to rehearsals, because have you heard this group? They are topnotch and the competition is fierce. The chorus has been around only since last January and I *do* prefer to take people who are here for the long run . . . did I read on your application that you were here on a Junior Year Abroad program?"

"Well, yes, but you never know what might happen," I smiled.

"Ah, now you're trying to bribe me," he laughed heartily, like Santa Claus. "But I'm going to take you anyway. You have a very pretty voice. I would study a bit to bring it out even more; there's a lot there to work with."

His young assistant, Gaëtane, met me as I left his office.

"Here is the vocal score for the first piece you will need to learn, the Berlioz *Te Deum,*" she said, "plus the rehearsal and concert schedule for the year."

It was after five o'clock and growing dark by the time I danced out of the building, clutching the sheet of instructions and Berlioz score to my chest. I nearly ran all the way to Place de la Concorde where I spotted bus #95, flashed my *carte orange,* and made my way breathlessly to an empty seat in the back.

My days were looking up. Being a new member of a well-respected chorus that performed with a high-end professional French orchestra made me stop wondering whether I was wasting too much time eating pastries and sitting in cafés. Perhaps it was the fact that I had to pass an audition to be accepted, or that the members were predominantly French. But belonging to it validated my living in Paris in an entirely different way than being in a program with clusters of American students invariably wielding L.L. Bean backpacks. Though Parisian skies remained dismal, I sat eagerly at my upright piano, learning the soprano part of my Berlioz score.

On the following Thursday night, I allowed myself plenty of time to take the metro to Porte Maillot on the west side of Paris. The Palais des Congrès was a massive conglomeration of stores, restaurants, and halls for international conferences. It also housed the rehearsal halls and performance venue of the Orchestre de Paris, Salle Bleue. Following the instructions on my information sheet, I hurried past the Boutiques de Paris, walked through through the stage door, and took elevator D down three floors. I entered an immense rehearsal hall and sat down with 200 people who loved to sing. I was home.

# FOUR

THE MEMBERS OF THE CHORUS were mostly young professionals in their thirties and forties, with only a handful of students my age. Many of the heavily mascaraed women sported diamond wedding rings and what I considered to be adult, coiffed hairdos. Dozens of men carried purses on straps around their wrists. I saw several people whom I had met on my audition day, and we cast each other little nods of recognition and congratulations. One, in particular, was Marie, a friendly, tall, slightly gawky woman in her early thirties. Short-haired and unaffected, she stood out from (what seemed to me) the other self-consciously fashionable women. We spoke easily when we noticed each other, and she became an instant ally of mine in the chorus.

Suddenly the rehearsal pianist played a single chord, and without a word from the conductor, the entire chorus began singing together in an impeccably rehearsed routine of warm-up exercises. First it was a diction practice, sung to the words, *"Popaca-tapital,"* on two triplet scale tones, and then the words, *"Le-Lac Ti-ti ca-ca,"* which changed the emphasis to three sets of duplets. I stumbled through, lost, and submerged in a deluge of sound.

Arthur Oldham had an atrocious French accent and made endless grammatical blunders when he spoke—a welcome relief from the typical French personality, which, I found, could often border on the self-important. The chorus sang the *Te Deum* with strength and finesse, having performed it already just a few months earlier. I was struck by Oldham's method of achieving an amazing *pianissimo* with the two hundred voices by asking the chorus to 'whisper-sing,' using mostly hushed air with only a little tone. I had learned my notes well and held my own without a struggle.

When the rehearsal was over, I could barely keep myself from skipping out the door. I belonged to something I loved. My name was on an attendance sheet. The metro no longer took me solely to random destinations in crisscrossing webs across the city—it now took me somewhere I was expected to be.

Daily outings took on a new sense of adventure. The following Sunday, I was out and about when I remembered the weekly five o'clock organ concerts at Notre Dame. I hopped on Bus 96 at Gare Montparnasse, and got off at Boulevard Saint-Michel, where I descended onto crowded sidewalks teeming with students and tourists. My pace quickened and a lightness hovered over my chest. When I arrived at Notre Dame, organ music was already reverberating within the cavernous cathedral, so I found a narrow wooden chair tucked behind a massive pillar in the back and sat down. I caught my breath and let the drenching sounds of the pipe organ fill me. A renewed exhilaration of living in Paris swept over me.

On Thursday night I returned to the chorus. I was enjoying the music when I was startled by a face on the other side of the semicircle. It was as if a movie camera panning casually across a sea of faces stopped and focused on just one: a young, striking man, around thirty years old, sitting at the end of the second row of basses. And the camera wouldn't move.

It was a sensitive face, radiating quiet intelligence. My fascination was less about his looks, however, than about his solemn demeanor, which stood out radically from the bellowing men surrounding him. I couldn't look away. At the end of the rehearsal he disengaged himself quickly, and was out the door before most people had put on their coats.

I thought little of him as I left the rehearsal hall, my spirits high and the last movement of the Berlioz, *Judex Credesris,*[2] pulsing in my ears. I darted through the concourse and hopped onto the metro home. The riveting tune that we had been singing could no more be contained inside me than the air I drew in and out, so as I took a seat on the train, I began humming the melody under my breath. A voice interrupted me.

"Ah, you sing in the chorus?" A thin man with long sideburns wearing tight, pocketless, polyester trousers and big tinted glasses had come over to my side of the train. He introduced himself as Dominique, and we chatted in French until, with relief, I reached my Louis Pasteur stop.

When the following Thursday arrived, I took the long metro ride out to Porte Maillot, walked the now-familiar route past cafés, the small post office, and boutiques on the ground floor of the Palais des Congres, and took the stairs down to level-3. As soon as I walked into the chorus room and checked my name off the attendance sheet, a man's voice startled me from behind.

"*Bonjour*, what's new?" he asked.

I turned quickly. Who *was* this guy? Aha, then I remembered. It was Dominique, the irksome guy from the metro. I didn't really mind chatting with him before the rehearsal began, as I still preferred making small talk in French to chatting with an American girl who had begun to seek me out each week. She would always launch into stories about culture shock, and I wanted no part of it. I felt proud of my integration into Parisian life, and flocking to other Americans destroyed my cover. Dominique reintroduced himself, and we continued to talk for a while, but secretly, I was disappointed to have lost my anonymity at such an early stage, and with it, my chance to spy on my new obsession, uninterrupted, from the privacy of my seat.

When our conversation came to an end, I sat down in the soprano section while Dominique surprised me by taking a seat right next to the handsome bass I had noticed the week before. I watched them shake hands. Basses and sopranos sat at opposite ends of the semi-circle, with Oldham, the conductor, in the middle, so when the rehearsal began, I had only to peer over my score to have an ongoing perfect view of this enigmatic man in the bass section. Even as I tried to focus on the conductor, his face was always there in the blurry background, drawing me to him and his secrets.

# FIVE

━━━━━ ⦿⦿⦿⦿ ━━━━━

*Dear Julie,*

*I thought about you throughout this past weekend. In fact, yesterday I felt like leaving Paris to go walk in the countryside, and I found myself in the spot at Fontainebleau where we spent one Sunday afternoon in June. It was at the top of a wooded hill, and we were sitting on a bench, and you sang me a song about clouds by an American folk singer. That's where I escaped yesterday with my books and my imagination. Overhead planes were taking off from Orly.*

*I listened to the Berlioz Te Deum over and over last night. I became nostalgic and angry with myself for singing this entire piece without noticing you in the soprano section. Finally, it was your smile on the stairwell that saved us.*

*Luc*

୧୨

The first concert of the Berlioz *Te Deum* came just three weeks after I joined the chorus. On December 23, I arrived at the Palais des Congrès wearing a vintage black satin dress of my mother's from the forties. It was the only black dress I owned, and I had always worn it at both Exeter and Wesleyan for the required concert black. It had an unusual, décolleté neckline, a fitted waist, and flared down to mid-calf. It never occurred to me that the teeny gold threads woven into the material might be a problem. When I entered the rehearsal room, however, a couple of women exclaimed, "*Oh là là*, has Monsieur Oldham seen you? I don't know if he'll let you sing the concert in that! Look, she has little gold *fantaisies* all through it! Just wait until the lights come on!" They reeled with laughter as blood rose to my face. Attracting attention was the last thing I wanted as a new member of the chorus. Once on stage, however, I saw that the chorus was so far away from the first row of the audience that no one could see me or my dress.

And when the music began, I was transported. Seated on risers just behind the Orchestre de Paris, we were able to watch Daniel Barenboim's communicative gestures and facial expressions as he conducted. This was thrilling for me, as Barenboim was a legend, and I had revered him for years. I sang easily and let the music fill my chest. Unfortunately, I lost sight of my crush, as a massive boys' choir was seated between the men and women of the chorus.

When the concert was over, tremendous applause brought the soloists and Barenboim back on stage for curtain calls. It surprised me that the chorus left the stage just as chaotically as members of the orchestra, rather than methodically row by row. Everyone was squeezing through the crowded hallways backstage. Some members were lining up in the stairwells, others streaming into elevators to return to the underground levels to grab their coats.

"How did you like the concert?" Dominique asked, appearing out of nowhere and grinning proudly as though he were personally responsible for it as a veteran member of the group.

I was answering him perfunctorily when suddenly my handsome bass was brushing right past me. His face was just inches from mine, but he didn't see me, intent as he was on making his way through the crowd. It was the first time I had ever seen him up close, and the effect was no less potent than if I had just imbibed a mythical potion. I trailed off in the middle of my sentence and followed this stranger with my eyes through the crowds. I watched his tall figure head for the staircase to leave, so I said an abrupt goodbye to Dominique and hurried over to the exit, too. By the time I started climbing the stairs, he had just made the turn at the landing in the opposite direction. As I looked up, he looked down, and our eyes met. He sighed with an exasperated "*bof*" as if to complain about the many stairs, and I smiled.

I was hoping that he, too, would exit at level -1, to take the metro home, but when I opened the stage door to the concourse, he was gone. He must have continued up until he reached ground level, undoubtedly to get to his car parked on the street.

My high spirits from the concert only marginally dampened, I headed toward the metro in my tweed cape, wrapping my white alpaca scarf loosely around my neck three times and tucking the ends into the collar without freeing my hair. After the twenty-minute metro ride, I sauntered home more slowly than usual. I let myself into the apartment with my unwieldy iron key, walked silently down the hallway to my room, and stood in front of the antique mirror over the mantel without removing my coat. What did I look like to that stranger on the stairs? My cheeks were rosy and my eyes glassy from the cold walk home. For once I didn't turn on the radio—it was too much of a distraction. Instead, I washed up and undressed slowly, crawled in between the sheets of my low, narrow bed, and went to sleep with the image of his face in my dreams. It was inside me, somehow, like a phrase of music so beautiful I knew I would need to hear it again, or a painting that stayed with me without my knowing why.

# SIX

—— ⬀⬀⬀ ——

*Dear Julie,*

*Yesterday I was at FNAC to buy the first symphony of Brahms
and there was a man in the adjacent booth listening to the Bach
Partita for flute, the one that you played for me in the little library
of your school building on rue de Chevreuse in Paris.*

*Julie, you are so lucky to have the flute. Because of you, the
flute was a true discovery for me. I never knew how to tell you of
the pleasure that it brought me, this relationship that you have with
music through your instrument. How many times I found it so
moving, so charming! It is a true scandal now that I can no longer
share such moments with you.*

*Luc*

൚

It was somewhat of a wonder to be arriving in Paris as a serious flute
student after the long series of uneven teachers I had had growing up. My
parents were not classical musicians, but there was always music filling our
house. My father, a lawyer, then a judge on the Supreme Court of Maine,

was a devoted tenor sax player, having played in big bands throughout Bates college and Georgetown Law School. My mother, though a tad tone deaf, had a penchant for finding the most enchanting records for her three daughters. They began with poignant little-known lullabies, then moved on to Greek myths narrated to famous works of classical music, and then to operettas like *Amahl and the Night Visitors* and *Hansel and Gretel,* and every Broadway musical imaginable. My sisters and I knew every lyric and tune, singing along with these records at the top of our lungs until our voices were hoarse and the LPs too scratched to play. These records were our closest friends, the soundtrack to our childhood. They immersed us in beauty and love, connected us as sisters, and imprinted on our DNA.

The flute fell into my hands at age ten largely due to a pedestrian crush my sisters and I had on a twenty-four-year-old flutist named Paul Dunkel, whom my parents were lodging as a favor to the local cultural council. Fortunately, I seemed to have a natural affinity for the instrument from the start. I knew I could get by with very little work, and it was just as well, as I was obsessed at the time with becoming a ballet dancer. Then came an epiphany at music camp, where every morning in an idyllic lake-side setting, we were awakened in our woodland cabins by Beethoven Symphonies broadcast at full volume over loud speakers, as if the pine trees had burst into song. I listened to my friends rehearsing Schubert Cello Quintet daily in the woods. Three summers of connecting deeply with kids my age made me leave my ballet slippers in the closet.

But good flute teachers in Maine weren't easy to find. My lessons had begun in fourth grade with a skinny Bates College undergrad who made me push my timid hand against his wiry abdomen, and then progressed to a lonely, elderly lady in Portland who cranked out lesson after tired lesson while remaining seated in a dark corner of her living room. By fourteen, and with more serious intentions, I attended the New England Conservatory Prep Department, when my parents were able to make the drive into Boston. There I studied with a talented, young flutist with a thick neck, greasy, chin-length hair, and grimy fingernails. As my lessons fell during his lunchtime, he would often pick up his gold flute in between ketchup-y hamburger bites to play phrases that took my breath away. His unsavory tendencies notwithstanding, my lessons with him were the first to really inspire me, but they were far too infrequent, and after I went away to Exeter, impossible to keep up.

When I decided to attend Exeter as one of the first seventy–five pioneer girls in a student-body of 800 boys, I was lured by the prospect of small classes, inspiring teachers, and the artistic outlets I craved. It was exhilarating to be on my own three years before college, living on a picturesque campus that was thick with golden-leafed maples in the fall, and tri-colored lilacs in the spring. Several mornings in winter, we awoke to a world that had been uprooted and dipped in molten crystal.

I was happy at Exeter, stimulated at last, but fraught with a deep sense of inferiority amidst so many exceptional students. Gloomy midwinter days tested our strength, character, and spirit. The 5:25 p.m. classes in winter darkness foreshadowed the dreary long hours of studying that lay ahead each night, which we countered by eating ample junk food at dorm parties in our nightgowns. By the time I was a senior, I was wearing the same L.L. Bean wide wale corduroy wrap-around skirt almost every day, adjusting it to the tightest or loosest button depending on whether I was eating nightly buttercream-frosted birthday cake sprinkled with M&M's or only salad that week. This irregular eating and dieting set an unhappy pattern that would continue for the next few years, and I joined the ranks of countless women who loathed their bodies and yearned for a waif-like shape.

I floundered in the midst of the pervasive drug and rock 'n' roll culture of the seventies, and felt equally estranged from the serious athletes who bonded over competitive team sports, like the statuesque women on the basketball courts whom I ran self-consciously past on my way to modern dance. There were other misfits like myself with whom I felt some rapport, and I was drawn to several teachers who were islands of humanity in a sea of Exeter maxims.

But it was music that saved me, both through the solace it provided when I listened to it alone in my room and in the many concerts I was asked to play in beautiful settings like the new Louis Kahn library. So I listened to my Joni Mitchell records and the brooding chamber music of

Fauré alone in my single dorm room, and wondered how life was supposed to make any sense during these angst-ridden high school years. And then I met Myriam my senior year.

Myriam was a petite, apple-cheeked French violinist whom I spotted at the first orchestra rehearsal and we became fast friends. She was the ninety-pound coxswain in our four-person crew shell, and, second semester, we shared a cozy double room under the eaves of the attic floor of Dutch House, a coveted, five-room girls dorm. Leafy branches grew up against our small square windows, enclosing us in what felt like a treehouse sanctuary.

With my new French friend, it didn't matter that I had never heard of the Doobie Brothers, or couldn't remember the name of the fourth member of the Beatles. Here was someone even more removed from pop culture than I was. At night we would walk back from the library arm in arm, singing French canons she had taught me, or sneak surreptitiously into the Academy building, delighted to find it unlocked. We'd sit on the worn marble staircase with only the silken honeyed light from the quad lamps outside illuminating our faces. Singing madrigals in two-part harmony, our voices echoed in the eerie, shadowy halls.

I chose not to attend a conservatory when I graduated from Exeter, which had ingrained in me a yearning for more than music. What was music but life, I figured, and what could I possibly hope to express through music if I knew about nothing else? I enrolled instead at Wesleyan University, a liberal arts college in Connecticut, where, amidst Shakespeare, Yeats, and Baudelaire, I finally started to have some serious flute training as well at the nearby Yale School of Music. But my teacher there was known universally for his neuroses, and adolescent tantrums erupted at the slightest provocation. Then came the summer of masterclasses in Nice with Lefevre.

Now here I was in Paris, fifteen months later, to study privately with Lefevre, however complicated it had turned out to be. To change my plans now would seem the failure of a chance not taken. So I practiced diligently in my bedroom with the window and shutters slightly ajar, knowing that my Bach Partita was floating out onto rue Brown-Séquard for all to hear.

# SEVEN

———∽∾∽———

*Dear Julie,*

    *Since yesterday I have been at Philippe's country house to spend the weekend. Faced with all these people who flaunt their happiness, I am like a sad and lonely outsider. I have been listening to music all night, isolated, yet tied to you. The wind outside announces the fall, which means it is my birthday in a few days. I wish I could spend it with you, walking through this beautiful countryside, feeling the bittersweet nostalgia that autumn always evokes.*

    *Otherwise just the little details of my life that feel so boring to tell you about. You, however, translate your daily events into a kind of inventory worthy of a Prévert poem. It's been four months since you left Paris. It's too long.*

*Luc*

∞

Christmas Eve was bitter cold, especially for Paris. Usually I didn't notice the cold, as I had learned to walk very briskly and would warm up right away. But this was different. The raw, biting wind sent a chill through me that only made me feel more alone. Many of my friends were gone, and I didn't know what to do by myself on Christmas Eve. When I opened my shutters and looked out through my window, it was like looking at a black-and-white photograph. There was virtually no one on the streets, except for one man carrying a bundle of flowers under his arm in a most desultory way.

I regretted that I had deliberately planned to wait until the day after Christmas to visit Myriam's family in the Dordogne Valley, so as to avoid their devout Christian celebrations. I hadn't expected to feel so down. Christmas was never a part of my upbringing. We were a non-practicing Jewish family, and we never celebrated any holidays, rarely even proper birthdays. There was just the unforced, unceremonious giving of unwrapped gifts at random moments throughout the year. Driving in the car with my parents, I would notice my mother fidgeting with something in her purse. Suddenly she'd turn around from the front passenger seat with a gold chain dangling from her fingers: "Here, Julie, can you use this?"

But during my years away from home, the winter holidays had come to mean a lot to me—Bach's *Christmas Oratorio* in Exeter's pine-filled chapel, the snow, the candlelight, the wood-burning scents of New England homes in winter. Celebrating light during the Winter Solstice. It was the pleasure and warmth of these associations that I missed deeply.

The only way one could tell it was Christmas in the desolate streets of Paris was at the Place de la Madeleine, where the windows at Fauchon displayed huge smoked salmons with transparent cucumber scales, animal-shaped marzipan, chocolates, caviar, and foie gras. People stood outside the store, looking in through the lavishly-decorated windows as they might admire the Christmas tree in the town square.

After calling my friend Jillian, we decided the place to go was La Closerie des Lilas, a festive, dimly-lit café on the corner of Boulevard Saint-Michel and Boulevard Montparnasse that retained an ambiance of old-world Paris. The bar area was intimate and cozy, enhanced by small burgundy sconces casting a low glow on each shiny mahogany table and *banquette*.

A dozen magnum bottles of champagne lined the ledges of the bevel-mirrored wall, and at the zinc bar itself, the shelves of amber whiskeys, ports, and cognac were lit from behind like Christmas lights. But the crown prince of the café, just within the entrance, was a conspicuous grand piano, where a singer held court each night, entertaining patrons with old favorites by Jacques Brel, Jerome Kern, Cole Porter, and Michel Legrand.

Jillian was a clever, fleet-tongued girl in my program who was always up for a rendezvous. Usually dressed in designer clothing, she was constantly getting into trouble academically, delivering late papers to teachers in the suburbs of Paris after dark, and often asking me to accompany her on these stressful late-night errands. Her perpetual name-dropping—from haute couture brands like Louis Vuitton, Versace, and Hermes, to celebrities and politicians—was completely lost on me, as I traveled in less worldly orbits and recognized none of the names.

I had yet to meet anyone with her questionable moral barometer. She proudly confessed that when she wanted to get seated right away in a restaurant, or was kept waiting in a doctor's office, she'd announce that she was Sidney Poitier's daughter, and subsequently received the attention she felt she deserved. She always had hilarious stories to tell. This time she was outraged because she had snuck a peek at her Danish boyfriend's journal in which he referred to her as a *"Négresse."* It was a word she abhorred, she said, although she regularly referred to the very dark Africans who tried to pick her up as "the Purple People," because their skin was so dark it had a purplish hue.

We ordered what we thought were appropriately festive drinks—Irish coffees—and, as we sipped through layers of *crème fraiche*, whiskey, and coffee, we talked to other family-less drifters at tables just inches away. I was glad for her company, and she was certainly entertaining, but I sometimes felt more down-hearted after being with her, as we shared so few real interests and values. I loved La Closerie so much that I longed to be there with a more compatible friend.

On the day after Christmas, my alarm woke me at six in the morning for an early train to the Dordogne Valley, where I was to spend the holiday week with my friend, Myriam, and her family.

I staggered toward the train station lugging my worn leather satchel filled with ten giant Granny Smith apples for Myriam (who loved them and couldn't find them there), a bottle of champagne for her parents, and some personal things for my week-long visit. The train took me away from the dreary streets of Paris and into the intoxicating countryside of the Dordogne. From the train window I drank in the breathtaking scenes of verdant farmland and sheep-covered hills and, as I got closer to the village, my mood began to lift.

Myriam, her twin sister, and her parents all eagerly awaited my arrival in the small train station of Bergerac. They brought me back to their 500-year-old stone house in a converted water mill, "*Le Grand Moulin*," which had been in the family for generations. There were stone walls, massive, open hearths, terra-cotta floors, and an airy country kitchen.

Meals were relaxed, festive gatherings around a pine farm table, where Myriam held court at one end with animated stories from our Exeter days. We ate scrumptious French stews sopped up with chunks of crunchy baguettes, and platters of skinless tomato salads drizzled with mustard-thick vinaigrette, sprinkled with herbs from their garden.

Neighbors from a nearby farm invited Myriam's family to what they called a casual New Year's Eve dinner, and they convened around an elegant table set for twenty with French linens and family silver. Every room featured exposed wood beams, French country heirlooms, and enormous crackling fires. We feasted on bouillabaisse and lamb brochettes cooked over an open flame. I struggled to remember the names and relationships of the hosts, neighbors, and the many college-age offspring home on holiday from universities in Antwerp, Toulouse, and Paris.

Toward the end of the dinner, the hosts invited the twins to sing an Ibert song, *La bercueuse du petit zébu*,[3] which had been a tradition at these dinners for years, and Myriam happily announced that tonight, since I was visiting, it would be sung in three parts, as written. Delight abounded. Then one of the sons opened a window, left the table, and went outside with his natural hunting horn. The forlorn, plaintive melody of his instrument floated into the farmhouse as we breathed in the sweet scents of mild country air. It was marked in our memories even as we lived it.

After the older generation retired to bed, I was the only one not twisting and twirling to music in a kind of jitterbug (which they called *rock*). I watched as everyone celebrated the stroke of midnight by jumping off chairs into the New Year, and we sat talking in front of the fire until dawn.

I enjoyed these lovely people, but invariably looked forward to getting into bed where I could be alone with my fantasies. As I drifted into sleep each night, I conjured the memory of that face in the stairwell. Who was he? Where did he come from? Would he remember that fleeting moment on the stairs when I returned to the chorus in January?

After very little sleep, on New Year's Day two groups of friends began at different farmhouses for a walk in the valley. We spotted tiny figures in the distance, met in the middle, and returned to one of the homes for tea and sweets. The countryside smelled of fresh earth and clean air, and ice was melting everywhere under a warm, bright, January sun. I was mesmerized by the scents, sights, and beauty of this part of the world and couldn't imagine any life that could match it.

On January 2, it was back to Paris at dawn, and as I shivered on a bench in the cold, empty train station, I wondered what lay ahead for me in 1977.

# EIGHT

*Why was it necessary that into my lonely universe*
*A woman traveled in secret.*
*In this life of apathy you touched me*
*Like a spray of water*
*And when you laughed on your toes*
*All others seemed to disappear.*
*I dreamed of an armor more dangerous than a weapon*
*"Are you French?"*
*Solitude was suddenly gone*
*I watched your hands*
*"I am a flutist"*
*Birds greater than wind no longer know where to alight.*
*Above you, your long hair flows*
*Into the abyss of our separation*

ᘒ

When I returned to Paris after the holidays, I was hoping to feel renewed. But day after day the sun stayed hidden behind dull, opaque clouds, and I struggled to stay afloat in the face of cold, relentless drizzle that permeated my very core as I walked to class.

I would sometimes make dates with friends for pizza on rue des Canettes near Saint Germain, or for an old Audrey Hepburn film on rue des Écoles in the Latin Quarter. But this required careful planning, as telephones were not a given in most of our meager student quarters. It sometimes meant getting on a bus and taking the unlikely chance of finding a friend at home. So I spent much time by myself, reading difficult assignments in French for classes, practicing the flute in my room, writing letters, and waiting impatiently for chorus rehearsals to resume. We would be beginning Beethoven's Ninth, the Choral Symphony.

When Thursday finally arrived, I again took the metro to Porte Maillot, and walked through the concourse of the Palais des Congrès to get to the grand rehearsal hall. Clusters of chorus members were milling about and discussing their Christmas holidays. I wondered how to come across as more sophisticated and less like a student, should I see my handsome bass again. Dominique came over right away, and dragged me into conversation. I even submitted to the double-cheek kiss the French use for greetings, the *bise*.

I had thought I would make real friends in the chorus, but there were actually few people with whom I felt any rapport. A love of choral singing didn't imply more common interests between us. Everyone seemed to know each other, and socializing appeared to be their prime focus for being there. The men talked about politics or exchanged heroic tales about home-improvement projects, what the French called *bricolage*. To my left, a man was boasting about the unusual green tiles he had brought back from Spain to install—himself, of course—in his bathroom. And to my right were the rapid-fire conversations of middle-aged women chatting about the upcoming weekend at their country homes, or a new leek and goat cheese tartlet recipe they had tried. I felt drawn to that one serious face in the bass section, the man who wasn't talking to anyone.

I was surprised to see that Dominique was seated next to my handsome bass again. His suit and tie meant that he'd come straight from work. With his pale complexion and boyish features, he reminded me of a young Irish teacher who had taught my Yeats course at Wesleyan. This stranger in the bass section never smiled, and seemed to exist in a world apart from the rest of the chorus. When Dominique approached me yet again before the rehearsal, I decided to use him to my advantage.

"Dominique, you know that guy that you often sit next to during rehearsals?"

He turned to look in the direction of the bass section where my crush was seated at the edge of the second row, looking down at his music.

"*Euh*, him, *oui, oui?*"

"Well, I was wondering . . . he reminds me so much of someone I know in the U.S. Is he French?"

"Oh, yes, *absolûment!* Well, actually he is *Breton*, he comes from *La Bretagne.*"

"*Ah bon*, I see," I murmured.

Later that evening something happened. I had become used to staring discreetly at my handsome bass from behind my Beethoven score, and was always able to spot him easily when he sat in his usual seat on the edge of the second row. But tonight his face was obscured by a tall man sitting in front of him, as well as a woman with big hair sitting in front of me. Only his shoulders were visible, then a bit of his hair, then his forehead for an instant, and then nothing. It was very frustrating not to see him clearly, like straining to hear a beautiful melody through the closed doors of a concert hall. When Oldham stopped us to correct the German pronunciation of *Ihr stürzt nieder*, I shifted my head and body slowly, just slightly to one side, to see if I could catch a better glimpse.

My breathing stopped. At exactly the same moment, he was mirroring me, inching to one side from behind the man in front of him, and looking in my direction. At me. Our eyes met for only a second, though from across a cavernous rehearsal room it was impossible to be sure. I had never seen him look up from his music at any point during the rehearsals. I wondered if I should smile, but the corners of my mouth wouldn't move. His face remained immobile, too, for that one long second, until we both returned to our scores.

I continued to watch him furtively during the rest of the rehearsal but he never looked up again. When the rehearsal was over, he slung his olive trench coat over one arm and headed with purpose toward the door. Gathering my things quickly, I began to walk briskly toward the exit, too. Just as I thought I might succeed in being the only other person leaving at that moment, someone grasped my arm and called my name. My spirits plummeted. It was Marie, the woman whom I'd met at the audition.

"You look as though you were running to catch a train," she laughed. I turned to see my Breton disappearing down the hallway and up the stairs.

"Do you want to grab a drink?" she asked. "I always like to unwind after rehearsals, don't you?"

"Actually, no, I'm sorry. I have to get home," I said, struggling hard to be polite, but sorely disappointed to have missed this chance. I forced a smile and said goodbye.

*Merde!* If only I could hear him speak, or exchange two words. It was the mystery of what lay beneath the surface that captivated me. And he had looked right at me, I was certain of it. I understood his estrangement somehow, and I wanted him to know. A week later, my frustration was so extreme, that on my way to the rehearsal, I vowed that if he were there that night, I would speak to him.

He was. My stomach lurched when I walked in and saw him from afar. I spied on him during the first half of the rehearsal. And then, for the first time that I could recall, he did not disappear during the break, but instead stood alone in the middle of the rehearsal room thumbing through his score. *I may never have this chance again,* I thought. Suddenly Dominique was coming toward me! *No! Stay away!*

*Bise-bise,* each cheek.

"Do you want to go up to the ground floor bar for a quick *pot*?" he asked. "We have about fifteen minutes." *What was it about French people and their drinks?*

"Uh, no, I don't think so, but thanks anyway," I answered.

*"Bon,"* he shrugged, and went off toward the exit.

Here was my chance. Nine steps toward the middle of the room brought me right behind him. When I tapped him on his beige corduroy shoulder, he turned around and was now looking directly at me. Transfixed by his strikingly handsome face just inches away now, I felt my breath give out. I regretted that I hadn't considered exactly what I was going to say.

"Excuse me," I stammered in French, "may I ask you a question?"

"Yes, of course," he answered in a voice much deeper and more resonant than I was expecting.

"Are you French?"

*"Pardon?"*

"I mean, what is your name?" Heat rose to my face.

"Luc Berthelot. Why?"

I wasn't prepared for a "why." So I seized the first thing that came into my head.

"I asked Dominique if you were French because from afar you look so much like a teacher at my university in the States."

"Ah, you are American?"

*Good*, I thought, a chance to go on automatic pilot and deliver my speech about what I was doing in Paris, the same one I gave whenever the question came up. I mentioned where I was from, my Junior Year Abroad program, my flute lessons with Lefevre. I had become confident and even cocky that I charmed people with my French. They always showed amusement at my chattiness and quirky, unidiomatic choice of words.

He was no exception. I saw him soften as soon as I began to talk. I was struck by his warmer facial expressions, which never emerged during rehearsals. But I couldn't look him directly in the eye.

"Where do you live?" he asked after a while.

"Oh, on a tiny side street near Gare Montparnasse, in the fifteenth," I answered. "You wouldn't know it."

"What's it called?" he insisted.

"It's really not very well known. Nobody has ever heard of it."

"The name of the street!" He pretended to be really annoyed. Utterly adorable.

"Rue Brown-Séquard."

"Don't know it."

We laughed. He was human. He was funny! I relaxed a little. Oldham's young assistant, Gaëtane, came over to Luc with a pile of large photographs in her arms.

"Did you order a photograph from the last concert?" she asked this man who now suddenly had a name. *Luc* something.

"Yes," he said, feeling for his wallet inside his jacket pocket, "but I'm sorry, I don't have any cash on me right now. May I give it to you next week?" I watched his manner and gestures with fascination.

"What about you, do *you* live in Paris?" I asked him when Gaëtane had left.

"*Oui, oui*, right in the Fourteenth. Do you know Porte de Vanves?"

I shook my head no because I had heard "*Porte Devant.*" He smiled since it was such a well-known metro station. Amused, he tried several more landmarks without luck, until he finally mentioned something I recognized. He continued.

"I go right by your neighborhood to get home and can give you a lift after the rehearsal if you'd like."

"Thank you, that would be great," I answered, dazed at this offer.

As we had come to an awkward pause, he opened his Beethoven score and looked down at his music. And then I saw it. A gold band on his left hand.

Suddenly we were no longer alone. Dominique had returned from getting his drink on the upper level.

"So I see you're interested in finance now," he said in a tone I didn't appreciate, although I didn't understand what he meant at the time. He tried to join in the conversation, but as Luc and I had stopped talking, the three of us stood uneasily in silence. I returned to my seat, at once stunned and disheartened since noticing the ring. *But of course he's married. Why wouldn't he be?*

When the rehearsal was over, Luc indicated with a small head lift from across the room to join him at the door. As soon as I got close, but still not quite beside him, he began walking quickly down the corridor, up the stairs, and out the stage door. As he was easily over six feet tall and took long strides, I lagged behind him, like a child with a parent. I couldn't figure out how to act cavalier and self-possessed while struggling to keep up.

The fluorescent lighting and piped-in muzak of the concourse was disorienting after singing Beethoven. Luc looked preoccupied and tired, seemingly unaware of me. We exited the Palais des Congrès and walked out into the unusually mild February air. On the other side of the busy intersection, we approached a little blue Volkswagen tucked into what appeared to be a highly illegal spot. He unlocked my side first, and after I got in, I leaned over to unlock his. I hadn't closed my door completely and he asked me to try again. Still not closed, he said dryly. Finally, I opened and shut it forcefully. And suddenly there I was in his narrow car, just inches away from this total stranger, *Luc something*.

He was very polite but freakishly reserved as we drove away from the outskirts and into the hub of the city. I jabbered on nervously without pause—first about my classes and what I was reading in each one, then about my Exeter years, my love of ballet as a child, the occupations of both my parents, and my holiday trip to the Dordogne Valley. And that was within the first three minutes. When I willed myself to stop talking for about a minute or two, we drove in silence until I started up again.

Luc spoke from time to time, but I absorbed very little, so mesmerized was I by the velvety timbre of his voice. Like music. He spoke elegantly, with perfectly constructed sentences, a connoisseur of the French language. After a bit he asked in an even warmer voice, "Why did you ask Dominique if I were French? Don't I seem French to you?"

"Well no," I said, "not from far away, not really. You look more Irish or English . . . in fact you look like a teacher of mine in the States who teaches a course on the poet Yeats. It's probably your pale coloring, your demeanor. I'm not sure. But now that I hear you speak, much more so, I guess."

He seemed disappointed. "Well, actually I'm not." This seemed to be an important point he was making. "I am *Breton*, from *La Bretagne*, and people from Brittany are very different from the French."

"How so?" I asked, sensing that this was something he was really eager to explain. Attention spread on his face while his eyes remained on the road ahead.

"Ah. Well, the French are Latin, like the Italians; extroverted, effusive, demonstrative; the *Bretons* have a long Celtic history, and share those qualities of the Irish—melancholy, quiet, reserved, and very tied to the sea."

"Okay, I see. And you? Are you 'tied to the sea?'" I asked.

"Oh, *absolûment*. I do a great deal of sailing."

"I love it, too. Not sailing, but the ocean, the coast. I am very proud of the white powdery beaches in Maine, where I grew up in the United States. I think they're the most beautiful in the world," I said.

"Ah, but you've never seen those of *Bretagne*."

I mentioned a piece that I had heard that day on *France Musique,* the public classical radio station in Paris.

"Ah, you listen to *France Musique?*" he asked, perking up, and turning to look at me for the first time.

"Yes, I never turn it off," I said. "I bought a small radio at Galeries Lafayette my first day here. I don't have any of my records so it's the only music I have, besides my flute!"

Luc smiled.

"You must come straight from work," I said, referring to his attire. "What kind of work do you do?"

"I am what the French call a *juriste*. I work for the Ministry of Finance in international fiscal law."

*Aha.* Now I understood what Dominique had meant when he found us talking at intermission.

"But I majored in both *psycho* and *philo* at the Sorbonne," he added quickly, as if I might judge him. "I went into fiscal law after that. It's just my work, my *boulot.* I have to work for the government for seven years to repay my student debt, both from law school and from *L'ÉNA.*"

Even I had heard of L'ÉNA, The National Administration School, the most prestigious institution in France, where all the presidents had received their education.

"What did you say was your last name?" I asked him.

"Berthelot," he said. "A pretty typical French name."

When we arrived at my street, I reached for the door handle before saying goodbye. I leaned in to kiss him goodnight on each cheek, just as

I had become accustomed to doing with everyone in France. But he was unresponsive. Only one of us was doing the *bise*. What did I do wrong?

Alone in my room, I tried to remember every word I had uttered that night. What an imbecile I had been! He must have thought me clueless and young. I swore that if I ever got another chance, I would be cool, casual, and strive to match his level of reserve. But it didn't matter. He was married, and of course, would only be a friend. Still, I didn't want him to think me *ridicule*.

Although the men and women often rehearsed on separate nights, the next Thursday was another *tutti* rehearsal, for the entire chorus. This would be the first rehearsal led by the orchestra's music director, Daniel Barenboim, so it assumed much more importance. I arrived at the rehearsal with plenty of time to primp in the ladies' room before the rehearsal began. I wanted to arrive *after* Luc so that I could make a casual but noticeable entrance. I tried to look ravishing, of course, or *my* version of ravishing, and just give the impression that I had forgotten all about him as I signed the attendance sheet and found my seat.

I tried this twice but he still hadn't arrived. *Merde!* So I left again, stopped to read the notices on the bulletin board, and slurped some water from the fountain. When I came back into the hall on my third try, this time his name was indeed checked off on the sheet. After checking off my own name, and turning to find my seat, I saw Luc talking to the rehearsal pianist with his back to the door, so my contrived nonchalance went completely unnoticed. Taking my seat quietly, I watched him from afar.

Before we started rehearsing, Oldham announced that he wanted to change the seating arrangement for the four sections, a request from Barenboim. Usually the sopranos and basses were at opposite ends of the semi-circle with altos and tenors in the middle. But now the entire bass and alto sections were being asked to stand and exchange places. The new seating order was soprano, bass, tenor, alto, so Luc was now just feet away from me, and I no longer had to struggle to see him or sense his presence nearby. I felt a palpable transformation of energy from my seat.

At the break, Luc wandered about the large rehearsal hall seemingly without purpose. When he finally looked over at me and saw me looking back, he mouthed, *"Ça va?"* with a slight lift of his head. Then he turned away. I calmly stayed seated, my attempt at playing hard to get. A few moments later he came over and we began to talk.

"How are you?" I asked him.

*"Bon,* you know, just tired, after a very busy day," he answered.

"What was your day like?" I asked.

"I just came from pleading a case—very boring. This morning I taught a class on fiscal law at the Sorbonne." He was bragging. *Sweet.*

"But you seem too young to have those jobs!" I said, not to flatter, just stating a truth. There was an endearing outburst of denial from him, objecting with a wag of his finger.

"How old are you then?" I continued. "Twenty-nine? Thirty?" He laughed, clearly amused at my candor, and shook his finger in protest, but gave no answer.

When the rehearsal was over, I deliberately took my time gathering my coat and slipping my vocal score into my bag. I looked up to find Luc making a steering motion with his hands from across the room, offering me a ride again. Dominique had realized that he was missing out on something, so he asked Luc for a lift, too.

"Hey, can we all stop for a drink somewhere?" Dominique asked, leaning forward from the back seat of Luc's Volkswagen. We agreed, and drove for only a few minutes away from Porte Maillot before choosing an unimpressive café off the *Périphérique,* the Paris beltway. We sat down at a table inside. Although Dominique was tiresome, I was glad that he was there, as it gave me a chance to observe Luc quietly from a different perspective. It was a relief to slip into the background.

The men both ordered beers. I didn't drink beer, and wasn't used to the concept of ordering a drink at 10 o'clock with two older Frenchmen. Sadly, I panicked and ordered tea. *Hot* tea. Parched from singing, nothing could have been less appealing. A huge pot arrived.

When Dominique mentioned his wife, I asked Luc casually, "And you, Luc? Are *you* married?" *Just three chorus buddies out for a drink.*

"Yes. But I haven't seen my wife for about six months now. She works outside of Paris."

*I knew it.*

Dominique launched into a long anecdote about his daughter, thus handing me a natural way to ask Luc if he had any kids.

"Yes, a son. Three years old. He is living with my in-laws right now in Normandy."

I felt dizzy.

"Doesn't it make you sad not to see your son?" I asked.

"*Oui*. But we have no choice right now since my wife is doing her residency outside of Paris."

There was an excruciating silence. When both men had finished their beers, I still had an entire pot of tea remaining.

I turned to Luc. "Would you like some tea?" I asked. "I still have so much left."

"Yes, I would, thank you," he said, taking my cup, "but I'll add some sugar." He dropped a sugar cube into the cup, stirred, and pressed his lips against it.

While he was sipping the tea, Luc said, "I actually have a question to ask you. I will probably be sent to the United States to work very soon, and I must absolutely find an effective way in which to learn English. Do you have any American friends who give lessons, you know, not too expensive?"

This was too good to be true. I could not imagine a more perfect excuse to spend time with my new charming Frenchman, married or not. I tried with every ounce of will power to remain calm and say, 'Let me think about it, and I'll get back to you.'

"I'll teach you English!" leapt from my lips instead.

# NINE

———⊶⊷———

LUC WAS EMBARRASSED AT MY quick offer to help, but appeared quietly delighted. He then repeated his urgent need to learn. Dominique was sitting forward in his chair, his eyes darting from me to Luc and back again.

"Let me know how it turns out," he said. "Maybe I'll try some English lessons, too!"

I immediately launched into explaining basic phonetic sounds that the French massacre in English, especially the "th," the "r," and the "h." Luc said he studied it in school for years but had always had a huge mental block when it came to actually speaking. "It's extremely stressful for me," he added.

"When did you want to begin?" I asked too eagerly, immediately regretting it.

"Oh, whenever you wish," he answered.

"If you want, we could just make a plan for the first lesson . . . maybe after all the Beethoven concerts are over, the Monday after next weekend?"

He agreed. I suggested my favorite place, La Closerie des Lilas.

"I should take down your number, though, in case something comes up," I said. I took out my little leather address book, turned to "B," and wrote down two different work numbers for him. We agreed that 4 o'clock would work for us both. Dominique had ceased to exist.

When we got back into Luc's car, we drove in silence for a few minutes before arriving at Dominique's corner. I got out of the front seat of Luc's two-door Volkswagen Beetle to let Dominique out of the back. He annoyingly hung his head for the *bise,* and I mechanically obliged.

In front of 9 rue Brown-Séquard, Luc and I talked a bit longer in his tiny car while it vibrated and jiggled irregularly from the small engine in front.

When we said goodbye, I leaned in to give him a kiss goodnight on each cheek—just as I did with Dominique—but again he was like stone.

What was I thinking? And how could I have made the same mistake twice? Sure, he was married, but everyone in France did the double-cheeked *bise.* In fact, it seemed to mean nothing more than a handshake to most people. I didn't understand. Well, I supposed, people were different. He was infinitely more formal than I was. Maybe he just didn't like me very much. It made no difference, I figured, except that it could be useful to know a brilliant lawyer in Paris.

The next day when I arrived at the rehearsal hall, I went to sign in but again took my time rummaging through my bag to find a pen. I wanted to scan the *Bass 1* column on the attendance sheet to see if Luc had arrived yet. Indeed, he had. When I turned to find my seat, Luc was standing nearby for once, and we approached each other cautiously. I knew just what I was going to say.

"I've been trying to decide what English books to use for your lessons," I said.

"That's very kind of you." He was *so* proper.

"I want to find something simple but not too childish," I continued, "and I think I have some ideas." He smiled. We chatted for a minute until we both went back to our seats.

When the rehearsal was over, Dominique was standing just inches from my face.

"I brought my car tonight, so if you want a ride, you can choose!" he said, grinning from ear to ear. I could barely manage a smile as I walked through the clusters of people toward Luc who was waiting at the door. Like the last two times, he began walking briskly the moment I got close to him, but seemed to relax a bit once we got into his car.

"I heard Isaac Stern with Barenboim conducting at the Théâtre des Champs-Elysées last week-end," I said, desperate for topics of conversation.

"*Ah bon?* Really?" he answered. "What did they play?"

"Beethoven concerto," I said. "Sometimes I buy a ticket for ten francs and then run up to the first or second row to an empty seat just after the lights go down," I beamed.

"Really? You do that?" he looked at me. I nodded yes.

"I always find it sad to go to a concert alone," he said.

"Oh, not me," I answered.

"Ah, not you," he smiled, his eyes looking straight ahead on the road.

"This is the first time I have ever lived in a big city, so it's hard not to want to take advantage of everything."

There were few cars on the streets as we drove away from Porte Maillot, and Luc's tiny Volkswagen sped quickly through the *quartiers* now.

"Do you know about the organ concerts on Sundays at Notre Dame?" I asked.

"Yes, I do, but I don't go very often," he answered.

"I went last weekend, and stopped in a famous English language bookstore right near there," I continued, "called Shakespeare and Company. Do you know it? It's an amazing place, mostly used books in English, with a maze of tiny rooms and quiet nooks with single chairs where people come to spend hours reading. I looked for a book there to use for our lessons."

He smiled. "What did you say was your last name?" he asked after a moment.

"Scolnik," I said. "It probably was a longer, more Russian version of that name, before it was shortened to Scolnik. At least that's what my sisters and I wanted to believe. We even told people that it must have been Rascolnikov, from *Crime and Punishment!*"

"Ah, it's a Russian name?" he asked, paying closer attention now, and taking his eyes off the road for a moment to look at me.

"Yes, all my grandparents were from the Ukraine," I answered. "What kind of work does your wife do outside of Paris?" I continued in my most forced casual voice.

"She's a child psychiatrist, but also a regular doctor, and is completing her residency." He gave all this information with a complete lack of involvement. I searched his facial expressions, his choice of words, his tone, for anything that might tell me more. I got nothing.

We drove in silence through the glittering city. Schubert's *Arpeggione Sonata* was on the radio.

"Once I spent hundreds of hours transcribing this piece for flute from a totally different clef before discovering that a flute transcription had just been published by someone else."

Luc turned to me, letting down his guard for a second.

"I have a couple of different recordings of this piece, too," he said. "But of course, I *would* have it—Schubert's my favorite composer, or at least one of them."

"Let me guess. With Brahms and Schumann?"

"Actually, I like them both a bit less than Schubert," he smiled.

"Then the B-flat Piano Trio must be on your short list of favorites," I said.

"No, actually . . . I don't know the piano trios," he said.

*What!?* How could he love Schubert and not know the two piano trios? All I could think about was how much I wanted to play the slow movement of the B-flat trio for him. It had been one of my single favorite pieces of music for years. That, and the cello quintet.

When we were only a few minutes from my street Luc said, "I thought I'd go down to Montparnasse to get something to eat. Would you care to join me?"

There was nothing I would have loved more. But I had to refuse. I felt the impending danger of what was happening between us, and needed time to step back, and take caution. It was as if I were dangling over a precipice, and if I wasn't careful I'd lose my grip and start falling through the air.

"I'm sorry, I can't, but thank you," I said.

A minute later as we turned the corner at Boulevard Pasteur, he asked if he could change my mind, and again I turned him down. His face fell. When we got to my building, I had the presence of mind this time not to try the *bise*. My hand reached for the door handle, and I looked at him. "Thanks for the ride; see you Wednesday."

His eyes and hint of a smile told me that he understood. I got out of his car, failing for the fourth time that week to close it with enough force, so he leaned over to shut it properly himself. We waved goodbye with a laugh, and Luc drove away.

The weekend was an unbearable wasteland. I thought of nothing but returning to the chorus the following week and seeing Luc again. The dress rehearsal would be on Wednesday, followed by concerts on Thursday and Friday nights, with the final one on Saturday morning. Reading my assignments for school was impossibly demanding in my distracted state: Balzac's *Les Paysans*, Marx's *The Communist Manifesto*, and Proust's *Un Amour de Swann*.

But what a discovery Proust was! I had anticipated a cold, pretentious novelist who would be impossible to grasp, especially in French. Instead I found magical (though challenging) prose on themes that meant most to me—childhood, involuntary memory, music, and the mysteries of the human heart. I was awestruck by his ability to capture the sensory, visceral experience of listening to music, the imaginary dimension of music that conjured inner worlds. He talked about a phrase of music, "the little phrase" of the fictitious composer, Vinteuil:

> "... But then at a certain moment, without being able to distinguish any clear outline, or to give a name to what was pleasing him, suddenly enraptured, he had tried to grasp the phrase or harmony—he did not know which—that had just been played and that had opened and expanded his soul, as the fragrance of certain roses, wafted upon the moist air of evening, has the power of dilating one's nostrils ... "

This was the music that Swann came to associate closely with his idealized love of Odette. Having first heard the music with her, Swann said that the "little phrase" that lived within him was like the "National Hymn of their love."

Proust understood that there was no greater connection in life than between music and love. This had always been my credo—that some music was the pure incarnation of love, like the *Adagietto* from Mahler's Symphony No. 5.[4] Heartrending to rapturous, over and over.

Our instructions for the dress rehearsal Wednesday were to go directly to the concert hall, Salle Bleue, on level one. The chorus would be rehearsing with the Orchestre de Paris for the first time, and chorus members had been told to invite friends to join them in the audience during the first three non-choral movements. Dozens of people were filling random seats in the cavernous concert hall. I had changed my outfit three times, and settled on a dusty-rose sweater dress and my tall brown boots. Walking with contrived self-assurance to a seat on the aisle of an empty row, I suspected that Luc might be in the hall already. Sure enough, just seconds after I sat down, I heard approaching steps. When I looked up, he was hurrying down the aisle to my seat.

"*Ça va?*" he asked. "I'm with some friends up a few rows," Luc said more solicitously than ever before. "Would you care to join us?"

There was something about Luc's body language that had shifted, tiny signs that indicated a more open and welcoming attitude toward me.

"Yes, of course, with pleasure," I smiled, and walked with him to another row much farther back where we rejoined his friends. He introduced me to Philippe, a wide-grinning, bespectacled man who right away began to speak to me in impeccable English.

"I understand you're going to give Luc English lessons," he said, evidently proud of his American accent. "What methods do you plan to use?"

I was instantly irked by him, and wondered why he was so invested in the matter. Luc mostly needed to lose his inhibitions, I told Philippe, and to practice conversational English. It soon became clear that Philippe's father was the head of a prestigious international law firm that was just waiting to pluck the young brilliant lawyer from the Ministry of Finance when his obligation to them had been completed—that is, if he learned English. Philippe evidently loved all things American, and Luc seemed proud to have an American friend to flaunt. I sat down next to them and put my legs onto the armrest of the empty seat in front of me.

"If she didn't do that," Philippe said to Luc loudly enough for me to hear, "she wouldn't be American."

Finally the orchestra began the Ninth Symphony. When it was time for the chorus to join the orchestra for the fourth movement, Luc and I walked onstage and went our separate ways. There was a great deal of commotion, and many people seemed confused about where they were supposed to sit. Once seated, we exchanged impatient sighs from our sections.

The choral movement began, and after the opening fanfare and recitatives, Barenboim became a philosopher, barely moving his baton when he eased the double basses in to introduce the famous *Freude Schoene* theme for the first time. When the tune expanded and the counter melodies of the bassoon and strings entered, Barenboim's face transformed to tenderness, his arms openly caressing the phrases. He led a moving rehearsal, stopping both the orchestra and chorus with numerous requests of balance, bowings, diction, and dynamics.

When it was over, Luc caught my eye and asked if I wanted to join him for a drink with his friends. We went with Philippe, his wife, Francoise, and an older man named André, to a café near the concert hall. Francoise reapplied her lipstick and redid her headband several times, avoiding any possible connection with me. In spite of Luc's efforts to include me, they all began talking about topics I knew nothing about. I felt unseen and struggled to feel their equal, especially when they launched into politics. I heard a few recognizable names like Giscard and Chirac, but it was no use. I perked up when they started making fun of Jimmy Carter, the Southern peanut farmer with big teeth and Southern drawl. No one would ever elect a guy like that in France as president, they said. They continued to carry on about the United States with assumed authority while I sat silently.

At one point, when Francoise called someone a *"mégaloman,"* Philippe spoke up.

"Be considerate, at least, of the young American!" he said. "Julie cannot possibly know what a *mégalomane* is."

Oh, but I *did*. In the eighth grade I had found a book called "30 Days to a More Powerful Vocabulary," and 'megalomania' was on one of the lists. Its English definition used words that were virtually identical to their French equivalents: "To have delusions of grandeur."

"*Aucun souci*, no worries," I said calmly, "Doesn't it mean to have *des illusions de grandeur?*" They were silenced, and for the briefest moment, I didn't feel like an imbecile.

When we had finished our drinks, Luc and I said goodbye to the others and walked to his car. It seemed a pivotal moment that he was driving me home as a matter of course without his offering each time. Once inside his car, I failed again to slam the door hard enough. This time, instead of asking me to try again, he simply leaned over me to reopen and slam it himself. His trench coat brushed against me and I could smell his skin and hair.

"When I was young," Luc explained, "I used to save my money to buy Barenboim's recordings, never dreaming that I would one day be singing in a concert under him." He changed the subject quickly, as if a bit embarrassed by this personal revelation. "What do you plan to pursue in the music world? Do you hope to get an orchestra job?" he asked me with a gentle voice.

"No, I don't think so. I mean, of course that could be great, but I think I am much more passionate about playing chamber music."

"But you shouldn't go back to the States," he added. "You should find French musicians to play with." *Adorable.*

We drove in silence for a while.

"Luc," I said eventually, "are you sure it isn't becoming a nuisance to drive me home after every single rehearsal?"

He looked indignant. *"Ne dis pas de conneries!* Don't be ridiculous! Are you kidding? Please, it's a pleasure! First of all, I prefer a thousand times to drive you home than Dominique, who always used to ask me for a ride in the past. And second . . . never mind . . . just don't say such rubbish."

After a moment I continued. "Having so *many* rehearsals this month . . . has been a luxury."

He knew what I meant and tried to make me feel at ease.

*"Mais non.* I'm the one who should thank you." He paused for a moment. "I'm very happy to have met you," he said without pretense. "It falls at a critical time in my life, and is more important than you can

probably imagine." He looked serious and his eyes were sad, staring straight ahead at the road.

I tried to decipher his meaning, waiting a moment before continuing.

"You know, I saw you once before," I began, feeling bolder now. Luc took his eyes off the road momentarily and glanced at me with intensity.

"It was December 23, after the Berlioz concert," I said. "We were climbing the stairs and—"

"—You smiled at me."

I nodded.

"Yes, I remember that well," he said. I was on a roll so I continued.

"After the holidays, in January, the night I approached you at intermission," I continued, "it was terribly forward of me, embarrassing, really. It's just that I really wanted to meet you."

He answered very decisively, "*Non, au contraire*, it was very nice. I just figured you were a friend of Dominique's, and as he wasn't there, *bon* . . . "

When we turned onto my little street and Luc's car stopped in front of my building, something was clearly different this time, although it took me a moment to realize what it was. Luc had turned off the car motor.

"Concert tomorrow night," he said sweetly. "I'm not sure if you know this, but there is supposed to be a general strike tomorrow and none of the *métros* will be running. If you want, I can pass by to get you."

Strikes by French workers demanding higher wages and better conditions were an everyday occurrence in one part of Paris or another.

"Really? That would be great, thank you."

Then, without warning, we leaned in toward each other, gently kissing one cheek and then the other. It was the tenderest *bise* I had ever experienced. Okay, now I understood.

"Good night," he said. "See you tomorrow." And his pale blue eyes had become liquid and kind.

# TEN

Dear Julie,

Yesterday I had dinner with Philippe. The ambiance was cheerful
until France Musique announced Beethoven's Ninth on the radio,
the performance with Barenboim that we both sang in. Everything
then stopped and I fell into a sort of torpor and melancholy. Where
are you?

Paris is so sad this beginning of February. Do you remember
February 1977, exactly one year ago? La Closerie des Lilas, Beethoven's
Ninth, the English lessons, rue Bonaparte, St. Germain, Buses #48,
and #92. So much seduction, aesthetics, and charm; time passed by
so quickly and transported us. In spite of all the problems that were
to follow, this was an unbelievable period in my life. Je t'embrasse,

Luc

My love sickness had assumed a life of its own, and there was nothing
I could do to reel it in. For the moment, at least, there were no decisions to

make. I *had* to sing in the concert the next day, I reasoned, as I unlocked the door to Madame Cammas' apartment. Beethoven's Ninth. *Freude, schöner, Götterfunken.* What else could I do?

When I opened my eyes the next morning, my insides churned. I was used to that sensation, the one that gripped me on the morning of an audition or recital. A knot would form in the pit of my stomach while still dozing, and then as consciousness seeped in and I recalled the events of the day ahead, adrenalin would disperse through my veins like a million teeny ants. This morning began the same way, and then I remembered why: Luc was picking me up that evening for the concert.

I spent the day as I often did: going to my morning classes, stopping for lunch with classmates at La Rotonde, then working on a paper, writing a letter, and practicing in my room. As evening approached and darkness settled in, I began to feel nervous and excited. I took a long, hot bath, which on these damp winter days was the only way I could really warm up.

The hot water calmed me. My hip bones were making more of an appearance than usual as I hadn't been able to eat for days. I let the soap run across my concave stomach. My long straight hair looked dry and undulating under water, like a mermaid's. But my body was still foreign to me, useless as far as I was concerned. When would I start to feel *bien dans ma peau,* or good in my skin, as the French loved to say. I was downright petrified of men's bodies and hadn't an inkling what to do with them. My romantic history had consisted only of unconsummated infatuations, ambivalent beginnings, and premature endings, so I had somehow missed out on gaining access to the complete set of instructions where sex was concerned. I hadn't yet discovered the erotic dairies of Anaïs Nin, nor had I ever seen or read any porn, hard or soft. I was plagued with self-consciousness about my body and filled with apprehension to be twenty years old and so ill-prepared.

I was no stranger to crushes. My first was at fifteen, when, for weeks, I passed a deep-eyed Exeter boy every afternoon on the way to my 5:25 French class in Phillips Hall. One day he said a small hello to me, and it wasn't long before he was giving me my first open mouth kiss with probing tongue on the boxy orange cushions of the Bancroft common room. Our kisses migrated to the private mezzanines in the library, empty classrooms, and into the New Hampshire woods. But I was a naïve fifteen and stopped his searching hands when he hungered for more. And although he never got farther than my lips, I knew our kisses alone whisked this sensitive boy away from the school, his parents, and the upper middle-class background he disdained. After a few months, though, the intensity of his affection for me and his relentless contempt of everything else drove me away, and I hid in a friend's room on the second floor of my dorm while listening for his knock at my ivy-webbed window below.

Two years later, still at Exeter, I spent my entire senior year nurturing an intense obsession with my thirty-seven-year-old philosophy/religion teacher, Mr. Fielding. Our classes were intimate exchanges around a large, oval, wooden table, and through our discussions, he revealed his complex, tortured soul. Every comment I made about "Oneness" in Eastern Religion held deeper meaning for me and, I hoped, for him. I knew every hour of his schedule—how else was I to orchestrate impromptu encounters when leaving a building?

One day outside the post office, he asked me to repeat something I had quoted by Kafka in class: *". . . that among the living, nobody can be free of himself. . . he must live with his secrets for the confession that liberates is impossible."* He told me that the quote had personal as well as academic meaning for him. I refused to infer anything from his words. In class I stared at his pouty lower lip while he challenged us to ponder life's essential questions. I had lucid dreams about having one kiss, the extent of my repertoire.

Then one day, during a March snowstorm, I heard my name as I passed the Academy Building after the optional Thursday ecumenical service. Mr. Fielding was leaning out the second-story window of his office in his shirtsleeves, and asking me to come up. I climbed the bowed, worn, marble stairs and entered his office, snowflakes still covering my hair and eyelashes.

"Please, Julie, have a seat," he began. I sat down on the edge of my chair, not daring to move.

"I just came from the service at Phillips Church," he began, "and I saw you there, too. Daniel's sermon about speaking the thoughts inside us keep coming back to me, and I knew I needed to say something to you." He paused.

"Religion 42 is a very personal course for me. When I ask questions in class and you respond to them so openly, or when we have one of our talks after class about an assignment, I feel dangerously at ease with you. I turned you down when you asked me to be your senior tutorial advisor on Aesthetics, because it no doubt would have ended in an affair."

Nothing could have jolted me back more to reality. I could barely register his meaning. He continued.

"But I don't know if I am telling you this now to make sure nothing happens," he continued, "or whether I am doing it to facilitate things."

*Please, don't say another word,* I screamed inwardly. The more he morphed from brilliant teacher to a flirtatious older man, the more I knew I was in over my head. If this had happened to me even five years later, I might have lunged across his desk into his arms, but at seventeen, this situation was so beyond the scope of my experiences that I barely registered it for what it was—an overture! I bolted out of his office and stayed away until the last day of school when I found him after our graduation ceremony, confessed to him how I had felt all year, and said a poignant goodbye.

When I arrived at college my freshman year, I was pursued by Miles, a wild, charismatic, graduate student with a penchant for making a scene. He found it amusing to let the world know that I was rebuffing him, and would yell to me across the dining hall, "Hey Jules! How's your hardline policy?" With a politician's smile and charm, as if rehearsing a platform speech, he spoke about human rights, saving babies in Africa, and his love of Ireland. Slowly I began to feel an inkling of attraction to him when he listened, teary-eyed, to a mournful Clancy Brothers drinking song from one of my records.

One afternoon he asked if he could show me his plants. Nothing could have prepared me for the absolute profusion of assorted greenery that besieged his tiny off-campus studio—large and small spider plants tumbling down in tiers from bookshelves, ivy cascading down the side of his desk, plants with heart-shaped leaves, pink polka dots, and a dozen more rooting in jars along his bathtub. Anyone who worked that hard to nurture plants, I figured, couldn't be all bad.

Besides, he was exceedingly persistent, and one day, after he brought me the first fragrant gardenia plant I had ever inhaled, I warily gave in to a forceful, unpleasant kiss. A few nights later, I thought we were heading to Brown University to see my sister in a play, but Miles drove us instead to his mother's Connecticut home, where, unbeknownst to me, his family had been expecting us all along. A nephew knocked over Miles' stray wine glass, cut his heel, and was rushed to the hospital for stitches. Miles was blamed for the accident and the evening degenerated into old patterns of sibling disputes. He got depressed and drank way too much wine at dinner, with the usual lovely consequences.

Even though I had been duped into coming to his mother's home, and was ambivalent at best about Miles, I was prepared to consummate our relationship that night. Being a virgin at 18 was nothing but a burden. But in the high, antique, four-poster bed of the family guest room, the agonizing act (which left an eight-inch blood stain) seemed to be more about his desperate effort to purge painful family dysfunction than about any demonstration of feelings for me. I ended my relationship with him shortly after, before any sexual discovery had occurred. Several times he sweet-talked his way back into my life, and a few times he even stalked me, peering creepily into my freshman dorm room window from a nearby knoll as I talked with my parents on the phone. My punster father would say, only partly in jest, " . . . and *Miles* to go before *I* sleep."

Then came the unfortunate incident with Lefevre, my flute teacher, in the garden of my boarding house in Nice.

No, it hadn't happened yet, not even close. Not only had I never been in love, but up until now, not one of my relationships had flourished, and I remained cruelly inexperienced.

I washed my hair and let it dry on its own, clipping some back in a half ponytail with a barrette. Personal ablutions were simple back then. I didn't wear make-up other than a bit of lip gloss and a few light swipes of blush.

When my extremely fine hair air-dried, several wisps slipped free of the barrette, framing my face with tendrils. After the fiasco of the December concert, when some of the women made fun of my vintage black dress, I had found a long, solid black, slip-style dress on sale in a corner boutique. Its zipper began in the middle of my back and went down to the bottom of my spine. Though I needed to wear a little fitted cardigan over it for the required long-sleeves, I felt chic and grown up in my new concert outfit. I sat on my bed sideways working on a paper, and then let my torso drop down, my feet still on the floor. I shut my eyes.

A few minutes later, worried about the time, I sprung to my feet and looked out my window. Luc's little blue Volkswagen was parked across the street, its front engine jiggling. Grabbing my purse, jacket, and Beethoven score, I ran outside.

"Sorry to keep you waiting," I said breathlessly as I got in, "I thought you would just knock on my window when you got here."

Luc looked puzzled. I pointed to the shutters of my large French window, three to the right of the main entrance of 9, rue Brown Séquard.

We drove without talking, heady with anticipation about the evening before us. Luc looked elegant in his concert clothes. His black suit recalled the night of December 23, when, as strangers, we brushed past each other in the hall after the Berlioz *Te Deum* concert, and I saw him up close for the first time. I couldn't take my eyes off him.

When we arrived at the immense Palais des Congrès, we parked and walked toward the entrance. I noticed our tall reflections in the glass doors as we walked in as a couple, something that made me feel validated in a way I was not used to. At the stage door, we parted. As usual, there were the customary warm-ups for the chorus in the rehearsal room. But rather than lining up in rows when it was time to go onstage, chorus members sauntered out at their own pace, taking random available seats on risers behind the orchestra. Oldham was in the wings reminding us that he wanted the new seating order—sopranos, basses, tenors, and altos.

When I walked on stage, Luc was already seated at the edge of the basses with an empty chair next to him in the soprano section. He invited me with his eyes to take that seat so we could sing the concert side by side. Although we could have done this any time during rehearsals, neither one had dared to suggest it. I sat down beside him under the bright stage lights, and could feel his right shoulder and thigh pressing against my left side. It was shockingly intimate. Soon the rest of the chorus members were filling in seats around us, and the remaining orchestra members were sitting down and beginning to warm up. It wasn't long before the hall grew quiet in the expectant moment before the orchestra tuned and Barenboim entered to great applause.

There was no way to measure the magnitude of my happiness at that moment. I tried to imagine something that might make me feel this rapturous, but nothing came close. The proximity of Luc's body breathing next to mine, our bodies touching, in the stillness of the concert hall, with neither the need nor the *possibility* to speak; the excruciating pleasure of knowing that we were feeling the same thing for the next two hours as we listened to music that we loved. My sensibilities were set free.

The chorus remained on stage throughout the first half of the concert while Barenboim played Beethoven's Third Concerto, which he conducted from the piano. After intermission, the atmospheric opening of the Ninth Symphony began, and I felt immense pride that we were now part of the performance: *Allegro ma non troppo, un poco maestoso*. Over the hushed, repeated open fifths in the second violins and cellos, the first violins and violas repeated a simple descending, two-note figure. Against this setting came the single sustained tone of first a horn, then an oboe and a flute, in fifths again, as if the orchestra were still tuning. The vibrations of the instruments coming up through the stage made my body feel as if it were resonating, too, like the sympathetic vibrations of a string instrument that responds to sound waves of other instruments. My heartbeat accelerated or slowed each time a phrase grew in emotional intensity or calmed to a cadence. At the most beautiful spots, I held my breath.

After the mischievous second movement *Scherzo* (which would always recall the Huntley-Brinkley news show coming from my parents' living room when I was a child), came the moment I savored above all others—

the third movement, *Adagio molto e cantabile,*[5] pure bittersweet emotion. A simple introduction by the bassoons and clarinets served as a prelude to not one, but two sublime themes which followed. This music stirred in me such deep sentiment—almost too personal, too poignant, to be listening to next to him, as if everything inside me was exposed, and there for him to see. Much like the discomfort of watching an erotic movie with someone you barely know. Our hands rested at our sides, our scores open in our laps, ready to use when it was time to stand and sing. At one point my left pinky inadvertently grazed Luc's right hand. It was like touching a power line.

The tempestuous outburst by the winds, brass, and timpani was our reminder to prepare to stand. But first, like a breath of fresh air, the principal themes from the three previous movements returned unexpectedly, in sequence.

The chorus stood on cue from Barenboim. Throughout the movement, from the mystical, prayer-like whisperings of *Ihr Sturtz Nieder*, to the exultant proclamation of the famous immortal theme about joy, eternal beauty, and brotherhood, the chorus sang with the depth of emotion and splendor inherent in the music set to Schiller's *Ode to Joy*. Knowing that Luc could hear me, however, made it difficult to relax my throat and sing out. I was also silenced by the exquisite timbre of his baritone voice. Absolutely professional in caliber. Like Dietrich Fischer-Dieskau.

"You have such a beautiful voice!" I said to him when the applause and curtain calls had finally stopped and we were walking off the stage.

"It's absolutely nothing next to yours," was his answer.

Dominique appeared in his usual perky fashion and asked Luc if he wanted to go get a drink, and I saw Luc agree with an unenthusiastic face. Both chorus and orchestra members left the building in clusters and headed out into the night, Dominique leading in front with some others. I looked at Luc with a pained expression.

"What is it?" he asked.

"It's that I would so much rather be alone with you right now," I said.

"But of course, me too! But what can we do?" he answered.

I needed no further permission. In a second I was running ahead a few paces to Dominique.

"I am so sorry, Dominique," I began, "I need to get home to finish some work for school, and can't stop for a drink after all. Luc is going to drive me."

*"Aucun souci,* no worries," he said, and I returned to Luc with an impish smile on my face.

"I'll never again believe a word you say to me," he laughed, utterly delighted that we were now Dominique-free, but also seemingly amused to discover this side of me.

We walked in silence to his car and drove away into the Paris night. Where to go?

There was only one place to go. I suggested my usual favorite haunt, La Closerie des Lilas. Despite my earlier hesitations about being alone with Luc, the emotional intensity of the concert had eroded my ambivalence, and there was no way to end such a sublime evening any other way. It was 10:30 when Luc and I arrived and found our way to a square table in the corner against the mirrors. We sat down at right angles to each other and ordered two glasses of red wine.

After a few moments, he told me that a friend of his had died of cancer recently and that he thought of him a lot during the music.

"Sorry for bringing this up," he said. "I'm not a fun, carefree type. "Many things preoccupy me."

"Oh no, I'm so sorry," I said, ". . . about your friend . . . what do you mean? You're not . . . happy?" I asked, regretting my clumsiness as soon as the words came out.

"After a concert like this, too many things seem too enormous, too important, to answer that easily. *C'est difficile,*" he said.

The cozy bar was full of festive, late-night chatter, French *chansons* at the piano, and the din of dishes and silverware from the adjacent restaurant. But I was only aware of the blood pounding in my temples and the steel-blue eyes anchoring me from across the table. We sat in silence for a long while. Gradually we leaned in, whispered timid phrases, and didn't stop for two hours. There was no contrived exchange of interests, background, or personal anecdotes from our pasts while wondering what the other was thinking. There was nothing about the evening that I had ever experienced before.

At about 1 a.m. we left, walking out into the drizzly night air. There was little to say as he drove me home. He turned down my quiet street, parked in front, and turned off the motor. Suddenly we were in a bear-hug embrace that was more a gesture of desperate relief than of passion. My face stayed in the nook of his shoulder and neck for only a moment, but for me time had stopped.

# ELEVEN

*Dear Julie,*

*I wanted time to stop. I had a premonition that you were going to call me, as if I felt your presence through the distance. My secretary enters. "Come quickly, Monsieur—it's Julie!" I feel faint. I run down the hall, I tremble and I have you at last. Then everything changes and the office becomes poetry. I hear our broken voices, to say 'everything' behind the banality.*

*Are you wearing the black dress that haunts me? Is the little black sweater thrown over your bare shoulders, only for me to take it off again in order to kiss you better? How can I say that on the phone? I suffer from being too slow to find the tone that might express the hurt, the hopes, and the sadness. But when you hang up, I hear silence.*

*Luc*

The next night, Friday, unfolded in much the same way. Luc waited for me to take the seat next to him onstage, and again we sang the concert side by side. Again, we drove away in the dark after the concert, and ended up at La Closerie without discussing it.

We stared into our wine glasses and let our faces become warm with the heat of the lively café. And then there we were, facing each other. Just time measured in breaths.

After a few minutes, Luc spoke softly.

"I no longer know myself. I can't sleep. I can't work. My secretary doesn't understand what has happened to me. That first night when you tapped me on the shoulder, I didn't close an eye all night."

I had no words.

"You cannot possibly understand or imagine," he continued. "It's been years since I've spoken to anyone the way we spoke last night in this café. I had my *boulot*, my work, and I had music, which saved me. I sang in the chorus, and I went to concerts. That's all. And I thought of myself as very balanced and grounded. Now suddenly, within eight days I see that this equilibrium was completely fragile. Precarious. False."

Luc continued.

"And then to think that in four months you will be leaving France."

I waited a long time before saying anything.

"Everything is possible," I almost whispered when I finally dared. I searched his eyes. "The problem is not that I live far away." I paused. "But that you're not free." He acknowledged what I meant with one look.

"It's very complicated," he said.

I didn't ask for more. But I saw right away that it wasn't simple. He said nothing for a moment or two, and then he continued.

"*Tu m'as secoué de ma torpeur.* You have shaken me from my torpor. I was living each day in a sort of sleep state, not happy, but not looking for anything else, until that tap on the shoulder. Then everything changed."

I trusted Luc blindly. He had made no attempt to explain anything to me and yet it didn't matter. I was filled with an overwhelming sense that there were no accidents. Or that life consisted of nothing *but* accidents. Was it the same thing? That one tiny event could have a life-altering impact on the future? The Butterfly Effect. I thought about how I had considered going home in December, how I had found the audition notice by chance when I sat down in that particular café on Quai Voltaire, how the sopranos and basses had been seated next to each other for the first time when Beethoven's Ninth struck us like Cupid's arrow. What could I do?

The café spun when I stood up—I couldn't remember when I had last eaten. When we left the café, it had begun to drizzle again. As we hurried across Boulevard du Montparnasse to his car, Luc put a protective arm around my shoulders. *Everything will be okay.*

Arriving in front of my building at about 1:30 a.m., Luc turned off the car motor. He turned to me.

"Concert tomorrow morning. Théâtre des Champs-Elysées," he said with some irony and an adorable half smile. We were drained by the intensity of emotion sustained for eight days now, and still another concert the next morning, Saturday.

"I'll pass by to get you? Nine o'clock? Does that work?" he asked sweetly. I smiled yes. The concert was at 10:30. Our call was 9:30. Only eight hours away.

He leaned in and kissed me gently on the cheek. "*Bonne nuit, Julie,*" he said, using my name for the very first time. To hear him say it redirected my blood flow. Waves of warmth and desire coursed through me. I was reeling.

Limp with exhaustion, I fell asleep easily. When I awoke, I could scarcely get out of bed without clasping my upper arms and bending over to steady myself. I still had no appetite, as if invaded by some lovesick virus. My lack of nourishment was taking its toll, and my insides felt as if they had dissolved. But it was also a strangely tranquil feeling, as if I were floating. As if the molecules of the universe had shifted.

Luc tapped at my window at 8:45—he had remembered which one it was! We hurried to his little blue Volkswagen and once inside, the rain started to hammer violently against the windows. We looked at our watches, then at each other, and began to laugh. We had barely said goodbye the night before.

"We are crazy, the two of us!" he said.

As we drove across the Seine to the right bank, the streets were empty and the city still asleep.

"We're very early," Luc said. "Should we stop for a cup of coffee?"

"Yes, great idea," I answered.

We stopped at a café near the theatre, one of the many hideous lime-green chains of cafés around Paris during that era that were oddly called *Le Drugstore*. Luc ordered an espresso; I asked for a *grand crème*, glad to have the nourishment of the hot milk, and we shared a croissant. When we left, avoiding puddles on the sidewalk and frowning at the foreboding sky, I felt less overcome with anguish than the day before, too tired from the week to think about the difficulties ahead.

The Théâtre des Champs-Elysées was a grand, turn-of-the-century concert hall on Avenue Montaigne. It had plush, red velvet seats and ornate gold detailing throughout the balconies and hallways. It was much more intimate than the gargantuan Salle Bleue of the two previous nights. The audience was closer to Barenboim on the podium, Barenboim was closer to the orchestra and chorus, and, as we managed for the third time to sit side by side on the stage, Luc felt even closer to me.

We listened to the first half of the concert, and after intermission, the Ninth Symphony began. This time the music was more powerful than my surroundings, drawing me away from the concert hall, from Madame Cammas, my classes, and even from Luc. I was thirteen years old at my music camp in Maine, and a hundred young musicians were filling the wood-beamed rehearsal lodge with the same Beethoven Symphony. I was filling in the flute melodies as I led the woodwind section.

But when the long, winding, bittersweet melodies of the third movement *Adagio* began, I was back. I felt a lump in my throat and that familiar but dreaded tingling in my nose which always meant tears were not far behind. As a child, crying in public was my greatest dread—my eyes would well up at the slightest embarrassment or criticism. I willed myself not to let this happen right now. Hearing these affecting phrases next to Luc suddenly filled me with irony; how could I let anything happen with this married man, father of a young boy whom he adored? I remembered some lines from Thomas Hardy's *Tess of the d'Urbervilles* which I had copied into my journal as an adolescent: *In the ill-judged execution of the well-judged plan of things, the call seldom produces the comer, the man to love rarely coincides with the hour for loving.* Even if I had found my perfect match, I knew that I'd have to walk away.

Half the audience arose before the last chord of the ninth symphony. Luc explained that these Saturday morning concerts were scheduled particularly for the blue-haired bourgeoisie who wanted a little culture when convenient but needed to get home quickly to prepare the big midday Saturday meal of *steak frites.*

"Shall we go get a bite?" Luc said as we walked to his car. We drove into my neighborhood and found a tiny parking spot on a side street near Boulevard du Montparnasse. After roaming a bit on foot, we stopped at Le Dôme. Luc leaned into the windowpane to glance at the menu posted there and asked if it suited me. Little did he know that I had spent long afternoons behind these same windows, with my huge *café crèmes*, salads, and schoolwork, and knew the menu by heart.

We sat down at a small round table in the second row, our black concert clothes conspicuous in broad daylight. The rain had stopped, and the sky was clearing. Luc ordered a beer and ham sandwich, and I, a Perrier and French onion soup. *Here they just call it onion soup.*

When our food arrived, I began to eat my soup, avoiding, as I often did as a habit, some of the bread and melted cheese that was baked on top. Instead, I dug my spoon underneath it in search of the onions and broth until finally I was left with a big glob of coagulated cheese.

"Someday I'll teach you how to eat onion soup," Luc said dryly looking over at my unappetizing remnants. This made me laugh out loud, and, as much as I was plunged into despair during the music, now I was feeling giddy and light-hearted. I started to talk with great animation about ridiculous, unrelated things. Luc listened with laughing eyes while he gobbled huge bites of his ham sandwich, dropping big chunks of baguette onto his black velvet pants without brushing them off.

I was recounting a convoluted story about a misunderstanding between the masterclass pianist in Nice, Alfred Herzog, and the school director, Jean Oubradous, when he interrupted me.

"*De quoi tu parles?* What in the world are you talking about?" he asked, as if I had been making no sense.

"Oubradous! Oubradous!" I repeated over and over, as if he were just being dense.

Luc was having an impossible time trying to stifle his laughs and swallow at the same time, his face turning crimson in the process. He couldn't contain his amusement, when, without warning, he blurted out, "I am incredibly in love with you; I just have to tell you like this."

The café became silent and pulled away, leaving me swimming in his words. I stopped telling my story, stunned by the unaffected timing of this disclosure. He didn't expect a reaction or anything in return. It was simply a confession.

# TWELVE

*Dear Julie,*

*The fatigue I was feeling was worrying me, so I went to see a doctor who ordered a mandatory week of rest. He found me depressed and tired. He said that if I didn't stop, I'd soon reach my limits. So there you have it; already the heart, now the body.*

*So yesterday I left for Bretagne to rest for a week on the Île-de-Bréhat. I realize now that I really needed it. My mother is not that well. I try to distract and reassure her. I spend hours giving legal advice to all the neighbors who want to take advantage of my being here to resolve all their little problems in the village.*

*At night I listen to music by the fire and write to you. It helps me to know you are out there, even halfway across the world.*

*Luc*

Luc and I finished at Le Dôme and walked to his car. The sun was starting to break through the clouds, and, as it was Saturday, Montparnasse was swarming with happy families. Everywhere people were out shopping, waiting in line for a film, or sitting at small tables behind the steamy windows of terraced cafés.

When we arrived in the same familiar way at 9, rue Brown-Séquard, there was little to say. The concerts were over, but the English lessons we had discussed ten days earlier had yet to begin.

"English lesson Monday, Julie?" Luc asked with an exceedingly sweet inflection. Monday was two days away.

I was happy that we had made this plan to meet at La Closerie before anything had unfolded between us. His spontaneous declaration in the café made my stomach flip each time I allowed the moment to resurface, but in my denial, I tried to convince myself that there was nothing improper about helping a chorus colleague learn English.

On Monday afternoon I arrived at La Closerie at 3:30, hoping to find a perfect corner table with plenty of time to take a few deep breaths before Luc arrived at 4:00. I had become used to sitting there alone in the late afternoons, as there was no better café for seeking warmth and respite from the damp Paris winter.

I ordered a pot of *tisane*, herbal tea, thinking it might calm me. Then I thumbed through the two books I had brought with me, wondering how in the world I was going to pull this off. Luc had made it clear that he didn't want to use a textbook, and preferred instead to learn in a casual, unstructured way. I ran my finger along the frayed spine of the worn, cloth-covered copy of Oscar Wilde's *Fairy Tales*. I remembered every word of a few stories, like "The Selfish Giant" and "The Happy Prince," from a childhood record of stories told to classical music. I could still hear the cavernous, slow-motion voice of the giant: "*How selfish I have been! Now I know why the spring would not come here.*"

Besides filling our home with music, my mother, a high school English teacher, had steeped her daughters in the beauty of words at a young age. I owed my love of Dylan Thomas, Yeats, the English Romantic poets, and these fairy tales, to her. There was one story in particular that moved me more than all the others. It was called "The Nightingale and the Rose," a wrenching tale of a nightingale who sacrifices herself for love by pressing her heart against a thorn to turn a white rose red, so that a young man can offer it to the girl of his dreams. I couldn't wait to use this story as a point of departure for our first lesson.

I was sitting against the mirrored wall in the indirect lighting of the burgundy sconces, sipping lukewarm tea and thumbing through the book when Luc walked in. He was stunning in a dark turtleneck and steel blue suit, an ensemble I remembered seeing from afar in the chorus before we had met. His olive trench coat was slung over one arm and he was carrying a worn black briefcase. That he might consider this a viable way to learn English was inconceivable to me.

He smiled a very formal *bonjour*, apologized for being late, and then asked if he could make a quick phone call downstairs to resolve a conflict for that afternoon.

"But what is it that you *do* exactly?" I asked him when he had returned looking relieved to have rescheduled his meeting.

"Nothing important," he answered. "I work for *cons*, for idiots." He immediately tensed up when he saw my books.

"Please, please not right away!" he begged me. "I am so exhausted from practicing law all day long. You have no idea how nervous it makes me to begin, you cannot imagine!"

"But you're being ridiculous," I said, realizing that this seemingly high-powered lawyer was actually panicking.

"I have studied English for years," he explained, "but have always had such a mental block . . . it's so difficult for me to lose my inhibitions enough to speak. But I can read and understand it to a certain extent."

"Don't worry," I said. "We'll go very gently."

Luc ordered *un demi*, the French equivalent of a half-pint of beer on tap.

He begged me again to wait a little longer, but beginning right away gave me a purpose to our meeting, and for once, this was my domain. I dove right in with phonetic sounds.

Luc's mouth was completely self-conscious; he could barely bring his tongue between his teeth to say "*the*." After a few minutes I opened the book of fairy tales.

"I brought a few things to show you," I said. "These stories might work, not only because they're simple, but because in every fairy tale, certain phrases are repeated over and over in each paragraph . . . kind of like *leitmotifs* in music. I think they might be a good place to begin even though they *are* just fairy tales and you probably will find them overly senti—" He interrupted me.

"Julie. Why did you bring this book all the way to France?" he asked sweetly.

I swallowed hard. "Well, of course *I* like them because they're part of my childhood," I protested. "But I have no perspective; I don't know if I'd like them if I read them for the first time today."

"*Fais voir*. Let me see," he said mockingly. I handed the book to him. He thumbed through it and came around to my *banquette,* so that we could sit side by side and share the book more easily.

I tried to regain control. "Why don't we start by simply having you read it out loud while I help you with pronunciation?"

"Yes, that's fine, but maybe you could begin first," he stalled, "so that I can get used to the sound of English in my ear."

I knew it was a ploy, but I agreed anyway. Reading aloud was something I had always loved, especially a story like this. So I began reading it very slowly with nuanced inflections, aware of the mellifluous timbre of my voice, now that I was speaking my own language, to a man I already loved.

"*'She said that she would dance with me if I brought her a red rose,' cried the young Student, 'but in all my garden there is no red rose.' From her nest in the holm-oak tree, the Nightingale heard him, and she looked out through the leaves and wondered.*

*'No red rose in all my garden!' he cried, and his beautiful eyes filled with tears. 'Ah, on what little things does happiness depend! I have read all that the wise men have written, and all the secrets of philosophy are mine, yet for want of a red rose is my life made wretched.'*"

As I read, Luc looked over my shoulder and I felt his breath on my neck. I stopped every paragraph to ask him to translate into French, and was surprised that he did, in fact, understand most of it. When I finished, it was his turn. He began timidly.

Yikes. It sounded *nothing* like English; in fact, it sounded just like French. I was demanding, correcting his pronunciation every few words. Luc worked hard, concentrating on every sound as he repeated the pleading refrain of the tree that could produce a red rose only by infusing its white rose with the nightingale's blood: *"Press closair, leettle Nighteengale, ohr zee day weeell coehme befohr zee rose eez feeneesht."* At the end of two and a half hours, Luc read the final paragraph of the seven-page fairy tale.

"It's just a silly little story," I said under my breath, fearing what he really thought of it.

"God, what a beautiful language English is," Luc said dreamily in French now, leaning back against the burgundy leather *banquette*. "You have completely charmed me with this story, Julie. Why did you think that I wouldn't like it?" he asked. He sighed deeply, looking tired and happy. "You don't know what a huge relief this is for me. I am sure that you will be able to help unblock me in English after all my years of struggle," he said. He leaned toward me, tilted my head to his lips, and kissed the top of my hair.

"You were really perfect," he continued, as we walked to his car. "You have no idea. I would prefer a million times to learn this way, gently, in our own way, without a textbook or serious *méthode*. I cannot tell you how anxious I was about it! Can you call me tomorrow at my office? Eleven o'clock? Don't forget!" And we said goodbye with a gentle kiss on each cheek.

I tried to find my direction and goals outside of what was happening to my heart. Blindsided by the certainty of love for the first time in my life, I barely knew how to function now. I had always wondered why I hadn't felt deeper affection for the boys who had pursued me in the past. Now I knew why: I hadn't met Luc yet. At night I couldn't free my mind from thoughts of him long enough to drift into sleep. During the day, studying was impossible. I would gaze at a page for thirty minutes before realizing I hadn't read a single line. I tried to force my mind back from my reveries, but it was no use. Added to this was the constant pressure to be able to discuss my reading assignments with Luc, as everything intellectual interested him.

The next day I willed myself not to call Luc right at eleven. I needed to convey a healthy, full life that didn't revolve around him. At 11:30 I picked up the phone in Madame Cammas' living room and carefully dialed the number I had written in my green leather address book that night in the café when we first discussed the English lessons. I asked in the utmost professional way to speak to *"Monsieur Berthelot."*

I was shocked at the warm reception I got from his secretary who seemed to expect my call. When Luc picked up, his voice sounded even deeper and more resonant than it had in person. He told me that he had given specific instructions to his secretary to allow any calls from *une Américaine* to come through, no matter what he was doing. Following orders, she had pulled him out of a *rendez-vous*. Was this a cultural thing, secretaries covering up for their married bosses?

"I hate calling you at work and interrupting your meeting!" I told him.

He responded indignantly. *"Mais c'est pas ton problème!* But it's *not* your problem!" he protested. "It gives me so much pleasure to be able to talk to you right now, you have no idea! Why didn't you call me at eleven?"

For most of February, this was the structure of our courtship: the phone calls every day at eleven if I was not in class, the occasional lunch near his office, English lessons in a favorite café at around 5 p.m., or, when it was mild enough, in the Jardin du Luxembourg or Parc Monceau.

"Please, can't we wait a few minutes?" Luc pleaded with me each time he noticed the English books I had brought with me.

"I had meetings all day and didn't stop for a second. Please let me just drink my beer and relax with you in French? I am begging you! *Je t'en prie!*"

I would try to relax, but my discomfort always made me bring us back to the lessons after only a short while. But they were not without fun and games.

"I have one book, a single book, in my hand," I wrote on my pad for him to read one afternoon at La Closerie. "Luc is not single."

It made no difference that the lessons were improvised entirely according to my whims. English conversation was all he really needed.

"What color is this bottle?" I said slowly, holding up my small green Perrier bottle.

"Careful now," he said in French, "I am *daltonien.*"

"You're what?" I asked, desperately hoping that it wasn't what I thought.

"Wait," he said. "Give me your little dictionary!"

He playfully snatched from my purse the tiny pocket dictionary that I always kept there, and flipped through the thin, crinkly pages. I watched with concern, knowing it could only be one thing.

"Col-eur blind . . . ?" he sounded out phonetically. Then back to French, he asked, "Is that it?"

"You're color blind?!" I exclaimed, unable to hide my shock. "But what do you *see* exactly?"

"*Bof*, mostly variations of grays," he said. "Reds and greens I can't distinguish. But I can see blue sometimes, a certain shade of blue."

I was shaken by this piece of information, and knew that I had just learned something that would never be okay. My mind spun through a multitude of things I now realized Luc saw as only gray: the infinite palette of greens in all the parks we went to, the bursts of color at lush flower markets, pyramids of strawberries and peaches and tomatoes at the fruit stands! The flush of color in my cheeks or lips. Was the world just one large black and white film to him?

"What do the lamps look like over there?" I asked, pointing to the deep burgundy sconces on the café wall. "And what do you do about traffic lights?" He downplayed it, saying that it didn't take a genius to learn that the red traffic light is on top, the green below. Finally, at his insistence, I dropped it, though I felt disheartened for the rest of our afternoon.

I would remain keenly aware of Luc's colorblindness as I walked around Paris. Now, everywhere I looked, the vast rainbow of colors that Luc was missing appeared more vibrant than ever. I began to smile at his occasional childlike mismatch of two bright colors, like red and blue, a pairing that a grown man would never choose. I never brought it up again. But I never forgot this, that he literally saw the world differently than I did.

# THIRTEEN

---

*Dear Julie,*

*Coming home from Bretagne I had the same emotion at finding your two last letters: one tender and poetic, the other mischievous and witty.*

*My health is a bit better, and I am more rested than before this stay in Bretagne. This noon I am going to have lunch at the National Assembly to discuss working in the U.S.A. I hope secretly that it's going to be decided quickly because it's now so much more urgent than it ever was before. I am assured that it will happen, and this will be the solution we've been waiting for. What I keep as my most guarded secret is my desire to preserve and cultivate our relationship, as it is the most important thing on earth to me. Nothing else has the importance that you give it.*

*Je t'embrasse,*

*Luc*

Despite my haphazard teaching methods, Luc's English did begin to improve. La Closerie des Lilas had become our habitual meeting place, and it had assumed a special meaning for us ever since those first nights after the Beethoven concerts when we sat across from each other, drenched with emotion and music.

Now, when we met there in the late afternoons, I would begin by posing a question in English and asking him to answer in a full sentence.

"What. did. you. do. last. night?" I asked, enunciating every word clearly.

"I . . . euh . . . make some work at *'ome* . . ."

"You *did* some work at *h*ome . . . "

"Yes, I *deed* . . . some . . . work at *'ome.*"

"*H*ome . . . "

"Yes, at home . . . and zen . . ."

"And *th*en . . ."

"Yes, and zen . . . "

"*Th*en . . . "

"Yes . . . *th*en . . . I . . . eat . . . *zeh* . . . *deenair.*"

"Then you *ate dinner?*"

"Yes, then . . . I ate deenn*air.*" Luc looked drained.

"What did you make for dinner?" I asked.

He didn't answer. My eyebrows went up, head cocked, waiting for an answer.

"*Oh pardon,*" he said, reverting back to French. "Can you repeat that please? I was staring at your lips."

There was no more seductive way to spend time together. Even with his declaration from weeks earlier, we had still never touched each other except for the routine goodbye kiss on each cheek. It was an excruciating, delectable, slow dance.

On Saturday morning I was out walking when I remembered our talk about the Schubert B-flat Piano Trio. I still couldn't believe that Luc considered Schubert his favorite composer and yet didn't know the sublime Piano Trios. I decided to walk down rue de Rennes to buy a recording at

FNAC, an enormous department store of electronics, appliances, cameras, records, and books. I quickly found the one I knew best (Stern, Istomen, Rose) and walked home with it under my arm, eager to surprise him with it, though I didn't know when that might be.

But that night at dusk, I was sitting cross-legged on my bed, wearing a soft, misshapen gray sweater and olive cargo pants which had become very loose. My hair was gathered in a messy low ponytail. I hadn't remembered to close my shutters yet, and was reading the back of the record jacket when a tap on the shutters made me jump. I looked up and saw Luc standing outside. There was no time to even worry about how I looked. I sprang from my bed and went to unlatch the window.

"Hi! I have something for you!" I said, scooping up the new Schubert record and holding it behind my back. I handed it to him through the window, shivering with nerves and cold.

He took it hesitantly, looking at once embarrassed and touched. "But you are mad; this is going to ruin you! I can't accept this. But really!"

"Yes, yes, of course you can. It's just a record! Do you want to come in?" I asked.

"I can?"

"Yes, of course." Although I was tempted for a moment to have him climb through the window rather than risk running into Madame Cammas, I told him to meet me at the front entrance.

It was the first time I had ever seen Luc in casual Saturday jeans and cashmere sweater, so he looked even more approachable, more adorable, more like a boyfriend, than usual. I walked him quickly through the apartment, and into my room. We shut the door.

And then there we were, standing awkwardly amidst my meager personal things. No living room to invite him into or couch to offer to ease normal socializing. No glass of wine to lubricate conversation. Just my bedroom, with its narrow, single bed. The only chair in the room was a minuscule, slender, wooden chair best suited for a monk (which I used merely to pile things on), and a round, frayed piano stool. I felt slightly embarrassed that aside from the music stand, vase of lavender roses,

Japanese woodcuts of calendar months, and my origami crane mobile, my room didn't reflect my personality or sensibilities the way it always had back in the States.

"I'm sorry I have no comfortable place for you to sit," I said, looking around, "but sit down on the piano stool if you want, or on the bed if you prefer."

He sat down on the bed and took off his jacket. I remained standing. As I had no record player, we couldn't even listen to the Schubert Piano Trios I had just handed him, but amazingly, Brahms' C minor Piano Quartet[6] was already playing on the radio. He looked self-conscious sitting up straight on my very low bed. He read the back of the Schubert record.

"Please, this is crazy. Lie down, make yourself comfortable," I said.

"I can?" he asked again. Such formality was endearing, and made me certain this was new for him. He lay down stiffly, one arm tucked under his head, while I sat on the edge of the narrow bed. We talked and laughed for a while about his day and the errands he had just run. We were aware of how ridiculous this felt, and yet it was difficult to know what else to do. Finally I joined him on my narrow bed, and we lay side by side listening to the Brahms. The slow movement had begun, and the long cello solo was exceedingly beautiful.

"They're doing this on purpose," he said, referring to the romantic phrases. His weight made the soft, thin mattress sink in the middle, and I had to tense my body so that I wouldn't roll into him. The swells in the music were becoming unbearable. When we finally dared to look at each other, there was no way to hold back any longer. We embraced forcefully but averted our faces. His face was buried in the nook of my neck, and his arms encircled the small of my back with genuine desperation. How could this vulnerable child who melted beneath my embrace be the same cold lawyer who drove me home that first night?

When our eyes met again there was no way to keep our lips apart, but he tried to, turning his head away.

"*Non, écoute . . .*" His eyes said that he couldn't bear to kiss me; he wanted it too much. But he returned to me and couldn't hold back now, kissing me deeply with half-lidded rapture. I was singing and weeping inside, with love, fear, and passion I'd never felt. My hand slid under his sweater and shirt and caressed the silky, undulating muscles of his back. I wondered how we had been able to resist each other's lips for so many months and how we would ever be able to stop kissing now. There was nothing more in the world for me to want, ever.

"We are mad," he said finally. "I tried to avoid you at the chorus those first nights." We lay on the bed in each other's arms, flushed, at once blissful and miserable, listening to the surges in the Brahms. "I tried. I really tried. But I couldn't do it. I just couldn't."

"I am not the kind of person who likes to do things just any way, any time," he continued, holding me, stroking the side of my cheek. This was of monumental relief to me, as the thought of removing any clothing right now would have been terrifying. It only made me love him more.

Now that he had come to my window once unexpectedly, he took another chance later that week. Early Thursday evening I returned home to find a note scribbled with dull blue pencil on a piece of paper wedged into my shutters.

*Thursday, 7:00 o'clock.*

*Julie. It's raining. It's cold.*

*I am cold. I've been waiting for you for over an hour, sitting in my car. I cannot seem to get myself to leave, as if paralyzed and frozen. But what am I doing here, on rue Brown-Séquard, if not to stare into the distance, hoping to catch a glimpse of you turning the corner in the dusk. Everything seems absurd. To wait in this car in this dreary weather on this sad little street—so that you might come smile at me for just a moment—and then leave to go home. Call me tomorrow morning. Tonight I will think about you. Good night, Julie.*

Where was I? Wandering around Paris somewhere, not knowing that anyone needed me or was looking for me? Nobody had ever looked for me or waited for me before in Paris. No one had ever noticed if I didn't return home before dark, or if I were wandering the other side of the Seine, lost, for hours at a time. I held the note in my hands. And I cried.

# FOURTEEN

"WHEN I WAS AN ADOLESCENT," Luc told me one day as we strolled through the Jardin du Luxembourg in the late afternoon, "I devoured dozens of books about class struggle, politics, and socialism; I was filled with rage about poverty and the humiliation that the poor had to endure. I wrote papers expounding my belief that no human being should tolerate humiliation of any kind. To me, the question of women's lib was fundamentally about this. At the Sorbonne I wrote a paper on the frigidity of women."

My eyebrows went up, waiting for more explanation. He added that he wasn't arguing from a sexual point of view but from a psychological one. He found women's acceptance of living without satisfaction to be a form of supreme humiliation.

"I was at the center of the May '68 student revolts in Paris," he continued, "and we were obsessed with the rigid French class barriers. My friends were throwing cobblestones and rioting in the streets of the Latin Quarter, but I was sitting in cafés discussing politics in underground cafés with writers, philosophers, and poets, even very famous ones like Jean-Paul Sartre."

We sat down in the low sunlight on two pale green metal chairs by the fountain. Children were sending small sailboats across to the other side.

"I earned degrees in both *philo* and *psycho* at the Sorbonne. Wrote my thesis on the mental illness of Robert Schumann. Supported myself through a series of grants and scholarships that I won along the way. From the Sorbonne I rode my *mobylette* to the Paris Conservatory on rue Madrid for my voice lessons.

"When I decided to go into law, my conservatory friends ridiculed me for selling out," Luc continued. "But I loved music too much," he said, "to risk tarnishing it with the business and practical aspects needed to make it a career. I wanted to protect it by keeping it an avocation."

He was successful in everything he did, cocky, even. So after settling on a career path, he then turned his attention to love and marriage: and why not the best—the intelligent, pretty, second cousin of the eminent Frenchman, George Pompidou. At twenty they were young and knew nothing about love. He was from a poor family in Brittany, and she from a famous political one, so they set out to prove to the world that they could transcend social classes. They married.

I didn't care *how* that happened. That part made sense. But I needed to know: what was the marriage like *now*?

"For years we accepted and agreed that our marriage was not tenable, that we had married too young, and for all the wrong reasons," he said, "and that we would eventually end it."

"But your son," I objected. "He's only three."

"Yes, yes I know. And I know this sounds far-fetched," Luc continued, "but a few years back many intellectual French women in the feminist movement were having children on their own, outside of any commitment of marriage or future with a particular man. Claire really wanted a child, and so although there was little chance we would stay together, she said she wanted to take advantage of my decent genes and have a baby. We had already been sleeping in separate bedrooms for some time as she is a total insomniac and has never been able to share a—"

"Luc—" I interrupted and looked at him incredulously. "People just don't have a child that way, the way they get a dog or buy a couch together. How could you not see that this would be such a massive mistake?"

"I can see why this seems so wrong and foreign to your idealistic concepts about family and love," he began, "but you need to understand. At that point in my life I didn't envisage much for myself on a personal level. We were each so entangled in our work—she in medicine and I in law. I had not been tempted by other women. I knew my marriage was neutral but didn't know that anything more could ever exist for me."

I tried to unravel these long explanations, but they went too far back into the hinterlands of our separate lives and values. Luc could persuade me of almost anything. But one thing was clear to me.

"I can't help thinking that in time you will only start to resent me if I take you away from your son," I said.

He looked at me and smiled.

"Why are you smiling?" I asked.

"Because you are a much better psychologist than I am," he said kindly. "But you're wrong. Look. Which is better for a child? To grow up in a home where there is no love between the parents and where the child will one day realize that his parents have stayed together uniquely for his sake? Or to live in turns with separated parents who have fully endowed him with security, intelligence, and love, so that he will have a better example to follow if they each find love in their lives?"

But I heard the way he talked about his son. I saw the look on his face when he boasted about Yann's deep blue-violet eyes, his intelligence, and charm. I didn't believe he could ever break his family apart. I didn't believe this could have a happy ending.

And the more I learned, the more I worried. One night at dusk, he recounted in a barely-audible voice a few more disturbing incidents of Claire's troubled past. I only understood bits and pieces of what he whispered in French, but I was pretty sure there was a self-induced abortion once and even an attempted suicide. I knew not to ever bring it up again or ask him to explain it more fully. I couldn't bear to know the details. But I knew it deeply impacted our future. There was more to it than simple irreconcilable differences. He was worried about her.

Luc and I fell into a regular pattern, and thankfully the evening rehearsals twice a week gave us a legitimate way to spend the evening together. He would pick me up at seven o'clock, and we'd drive across the city in silence, knowing that the next few hours were ours. Walking into the rehearsal hall together past other chorus members, we would separate once we reached our sections. No one knew our story, but it was clear that many had noticed that Luc, who had always remained utterly detached from everyone, was now showing up each time with the twenty-year-old American girl. A few of the women gave me cold stares up and down when I passed by with him, clearly baffled at why he would go for someone like me when they had tried without luck to draw his interest. When I found myself in an elevator with a woman with whom I had never exchanged a single word or kind look, she asked me in a very pointed, unpleasant tone, "Are you leaving Paris *definitively* at the end of this school year?" Another time, my friend Marie deliberately snubbed me as we passed in the hallway.

"What's wrong?" I asked her when I was certain it wasn't my imagination.

"I don't approve of what you are doing," she answered.

"But you know absolutely nothing about it," I replied, annoyed that she was judging me without any of the facts. Marie had no information about the status of Luc's marriage, nor about our relationship. Was it simply his wedding ring that gave him away?

"All I can say is that I wouldn't appreciate it if someone did this to me," she said.

Her reaction bothered me, of course, and I wanted to explain that it wasn't my nature to get entangled in a clichéd love triangle with a married man. That he was *essentially* single.

But when I told Luc, we laughed about it and called Marie a busybody, and it only reinforced our feeling of elitism. No one understood our situation; no one could take away the sheer bliss we shared in each other's company.

Every day I was struck by the lunacy that a man like Luc loved me. It never occurred to me to want more than he could give me, because nothing in my life had ever given me as much. Only on occasion did I remember that he wasn't free for me to love, and then the light would recede from my face, like a summer thunderstorm that creeps up without warning, with no time to run inside.

Once we were sitting in his car outside my building when he noticed this change.

"What are you thinking?" he asked.

"I'm scared," I said pensively. "I cannot believe I walked into this with my eyes wide open . . . I should have been more careful . . . I should have protected myself."

There was a long silence. "I find that sweet," he said finally, "because it implies that there is something precious to protect." I looked at him, waiting for anything to reassure me.

"I understand," he said. But he added nothing else. I began to see that there was a serious problem.

Behind closed shutters, the first two windows in Madame Cammas' apartment were lit; the third one, mine, was dark. I imagined Madame Cammas inside, sitting in a heap of wrinkled clothes in a corner of her living room with her tray of soup, smelly ripe cheeses, and baguette. Her baggy eyelids would be drooped over eyes fixed wearily on the blue light of the French *télé*. Poor Madame Cammas. Her life was companionless and dreary, yet I felt little sympathy for her. Each time I came home late at night, turning my key in the door as quietly as I could, she would appear like a ghost in the doorway of the living room as I walked past it. She would glare at me and announce:

"You had *three* calls tonight!"

"I'm so sorry. Did anyone leave a name?" I'd ask.

*"NON!"*

I was prepared to hear her reprimand and lecture me, to say this had to stop. That yes, I was a nice girl when I arrived, a young American girl. Innocent, sweet! But now I was getting phone calls, sometimes from boys, and laughing with a man on my bed behind my closed bedroom door. It had to stop. She didn't want a tenant like me.

But there were no words, just a cold stare after I apologized briefly and walked past her into my room. So Luc and I would sit in the darkness of his car, with only the street lamps casting a silver glow on our faces. He would turn off the car motor and a heavenly silence would envelope us. I didn't want to leave his car. He didn't want to let me go. I'd stare out at the quiet street; his eyes would be fixed blankly on his steering wheel. Finally he would turn to look at me one last time with eyes that made my insides go wobbly.

"Call me tomorrow? Eleven o'clock?"

I nodded yes, kissing him softly on one cheek, then the other, forcing myself to open the car door, knowing that facing Madame Cammas was all that awaited me.

# FIFTEEN

*She worries about his absent moods,*
*she dreams of a deeper communication*
*She dreams of springtime, of kisses*
*Is he sick or tired?*
       *Is he more unhappy than usual?*
*He doesn't answer; the bus continues its route*
*And yet everything moves in him,*
*Her light, Her warmth*
*And in his absent eyes her charms gather*
*Light overflows from eyes that look into mine.*
*He makes dull gestures,*
*Aware that he'll forget nothing.*
*And then, suddenly, he no longer thinks.*
*He feels in this desert which inhabits him*
*That she is embracing him,*
*With words, with kisses*

                                     *Luc*

Luc and I had made a plan to meet early one Saturday morning for an English lesson. I thought it would be a nice change to offer him coffee in my room instead of meeting in a café.

I kept nothing on my designated kitchen shelf, so I awoke early to buy ground coffee, a couple of mini croissants, some strawberries, and a box of five-hundred sugar cubes for the two that I knew Luc would need for his coffee. Irrationally anxious about this small act of hospitality, I rushed into the kitchen to unpack the items and heat the milk. When the milk seemed warm and began to foam, I lifted the pot off the gas, but the handle was loose and caused it to swivel violently side to side, sending hot milk flying all over the stove, the floor, and my clothes. In full panic mode, I tried to wipe up the mess, make the coffee, pour more milk into the pot, and stuff my soiled clothes into the armoire. I pulled a clean sweater over my head and had barely managed to push down the plunger of the coffee maker when Luc knocked at my window.

As he often did these days, Luc hoisted himself over the wide window ledge to enter into my room. In anticipation of this breakfast invitation, I had borrowed a beautiful, small, oval wooden table from a photographer friend, Paula, who lived in a much nicer studio than most of the students I knew. The radio was on as I invited Luc to sit down at the table. I sat on the hard straight monk chair and Luc, the round, velvet piano stool. The coffee tasted horrific. Luc sipped it politely and told me it was good.

Suddenly the crystal clear voice of a boy soprano came over the radio, rising eloquently over the accompaniment of a treble chorus.

"*C'est moi,*" he said, nonchalantly, perking up his ears and indicating the radio.

"WHAT!??"

"That's me," he said again, "singing . . . on the radio. That's me." And then he explained.

"When I was about eight years old, my uncle took me to audition for *Les Petits Chanteurs à la Croix de Bois,* a well-known boys' choir which toured the world giving concerts. I had never been exposed to music before in my home, but for some reason I had a good voice and was accepted. I began living with a group of young boys and three Jesuit priests in Brittany, where we rehearsed and received our education. I was their soloist until the age of twelve, when my voice began to change. We went everywhere—to Italy, Russia, and Japan. We sang for the Queen of England when she arrived in Paris; and we sang in Notre Dame during the Christmas services, all the time with me as soloist."

I motioned for him to hush while I listened to his astonishingly pure timbre.

"These years with the choir saved me from a miserable childhood," he continued. "The music and education gave me my sense of poetry and aesthetics. I was the smallest boy in the choir. One of the monsignors and I were very close, and we would have philosophical discussions about what I thought the texts of the music meant. This piece in particular, which you're hearing now. I remember discussing it with him. It's called *La Nuit*[7] by Jean-Philippe Rameau.[3]"

"But how could that be you?" I searched his face with disbelief. His soprano voice was flawless and clear, shimmering bell-like above the accompaniment of the chorus, and, with its delicate vibrato, expressive beyond a child's years. I was awestruck. It clearly moved him, too, and he didn't deny that it was good.

"It's no longer me, of course," he said. "Really, I didn't even know this recording existed, and I haven't heard it since the day I sang it," he said with his usual nonchalance.

"I was a sad little boy; we were very poor. My mother was very ill and almost died after I was born. I was passed from nurse to nurse my first years. My father worked hard and there was no sense of family. In those days, the government paid nurses to help poor families raise their children. I hated these women and was very disobedient and uncooperative. Once I deliberately spilled hot soup on one of them and waited at the door for my father to scold me."

I began to understand who Luc was, how injured he was as a child, and why he had built up such impenetrable walls to protect himself from misery. I wanted to wrap the little nine-year-old boy in my arms, envelop him with love, and rock him until some of it reached his buried heart.

# SIXTEEN

Dear Julie,

*I was dozing in the sun when they announced on France Musique the duo aria from Mozart's Magic Flute that we once sang together. From the very first moments, a dagger went into me. Do you remember when we sang this soprano/baritone duo together, sitting next to each other, sight-reading at the piano of that sorcerer, Madame Cammas? Horrible.*

*Last week I sorted through papers in my office. I read all the notes that you wrote to me when you lived in Paris, and they filled me with such emotion. I often pass by rue Brown-Séquard and look at your window, hoping to see you furtively appear at the sound of my car. Where are you?*

*Luc*

"Let me come see *Death in Venice* with you," Luc said to me one day, as we sat in Closerie at our habitual table in the corner. It was an assignment for my film class, in which we were studying the films of Luciano Visconti.

"But it's only showing during the day and at only one theater, Le Champo," I answered, after consulting my *Pariscope*, the Parisian guide for all films, concerts, plays, and exhibits.

"It's such a beautiful film," he said. "I want to see it with you. I can leave work early."

The next day at 5:10, we met in front of the small movie theater in the Latin Quarter on rue des Écoles. Luc told me that this was one of the most famous arthouse movie theaters in Paris, where generations of students, directors, and cinema lovers learned about the art of filmmaking. *Death in Venice,* based on the novel by Thomas Mann, was beautifully sensuous, full of irrational yearning, scenes of Venice, and the heart-rending music of Mahler. We had never sat together in a darkened movie theater, and this one was very special—small and intimate, with extremely comfortable, plush, velour seats. And we were virtually alone. Throughout the film Luc explored my hands, delicately tracing each of my fingers, veins, and knuckles, and making tiny soft caresses in a hundred different ways. With each stroke he was undressing me in the dark, sending waves of pleasure through my body, as if for the first time.

Our morning phone calls at 11 o'clock would determine whether I was to meet him in a café later that afternoon, or expect a tap on my window after his work day. One early evening, Luc and I sat side by side at the upright piano in Madame Cammas' apartment, sight-singing a soprano-bass duet, *Bei Männern,*[8] from *The Magic Flute.* I clumsily played the chords of the accompaniment as he tried to play the notes of his bass part while he sang. We bumped shoulders and laughed at our lack of talent. I got up and lay down on the bed, while Luc stayed there, picking out the chords of a song by Jean Ferrat, a French folk singer he had known well when he was a student. Under his breath he sang *Ma France,*[9] a song inspired by the widespread protests in France, in May of 1968. Luc had helped Ferrat write the lyrics, a series of vignettes about the beauty of France—the lavender of Provence, and the cliffs of Brittany; the poetry of Éluard, and the paintings of Picasso—*artistes prophètes,* who will never stop decrying social injustice. It was a passionate nationalistic song, exuding both a deep abiding love of

France and a condemnation of its leaders. I watched and listened from the bed, moved to be peeking into his life before I met him.

As 7:30 approached, Luc swiveled on the piano stool to look at me. "It is seven-thirty, Julie. Generally, at this hour I would go home and make something for dinner. If you'd like to come with me, we can eat dinner together and I can play some of the records for you that we talked about. Tomorrow night the apartment will be full of people: Claire's brother and his friend are coming from Normandy to use the apartment. Tonight we'll be *tranquille,* alone."

At first I refused. This was a line I wouldn't cross, being in the apartment that he shared with his wife, even though they were practically separated. I said goodbye to him and planned to get some work done.

A minute later I could find no logic in my decision. Whether I went with him or not wouldn't change a thing. What would it prove *now* to show restraint? Would it erase the fact that I was already deeply entangled, past the point of no return? Wasn't this what one might call "closing the barn door after the horse got out?" I ran out of Madame Cammas' apartment and waved him down before he drove away.

"What I love about you, Mademoiselle Scolnik, is your sense of work ethic, your strength of will, your discipline," he said dryly with a half-smile.

Arriving on rue Hallé in the fourteenth *arrondissement,* I followed him through the garage and into the elevator of his modern apartment building. I didn't know that ugly buildings like this even *existed* in Paris. We got off at the seventh floor, and I watched uneasily as he unlocked the door to his small apartment.

"You ok?" he asked, noticing my discomfort.

We stepped inside.

Luc quickly closed the doors to two tiny bedrooms, inside each of which was a small single bed. I was taken aback at how stark and devoid of decor the apartment was. It was undeniably a place for Luc and Claire to simply eat and sleep. *Separately.* It was difficult for me to understand how anyone could live like this, as I had always surrounded myself with lovely things to look at, even when as a child my little treasures cost practically nothing—Impressionist postcards taped over my top bunk bed at music camp, ceramic frogs, incense holders, and miniature candlesticks nestled into the wood beams. Throughout my high school and college years, my dorm rooms were decorated with more sophisticated art prints, origami mobiles, candles on the windowsill, dried flowers, and crystal prisms hung in sunlit windows that beamed rainbows onto the walls, like in my favorite childhood movie, *Pollyanna.*

A beige, boxy, sectional sofa was just inside the entrance, and there was a record player in the corner. I looked around the room, noting that the sole exceptions to the non-existent furnishings were an avocado plant next to the stereo and a portrait of a woman on the wall. It made me uneasy, as if to remind me that this wasn't just Luc's apartment. After putting on some early madrigals recorded by a choir he sang with during his Sorbonne years, he went into the kitchen to make us something to eat, and told me to make myself comfortable. I pulled off my boots and curled my feet underneath me on the couch, desperate to feel cozy. The music was calming, and connected me to Luc. Listening to music, I realized, was how Luc created the warmth he needed. He put together a simple meal of sliced roast beef and salad and came into the living room carrying a tray with two plates of food, two glasses of wine, and a baguette, and placed it on the coffee table.

I lit two candles. We ate quietly while listening to more music. I was happy to be eating that way with him, to be sharing a meal so unpretentiously without the artificial romance of a fancy restaurant. He spent little much money in general, and virtually nothing on me. I wouldn't have minded a small token of affection once in a while, but in a way, it reassured me that he didn't fit the stereotype of the married, philandering Frenchman. I never once felt that I was being used; in fact, there had been neither gifts nor sexual favors—though I suspected that this was about to change—just the intense pleasure of each other's company. I never doubted his feelings for me.

Luc sat back, sighed, and took his wine glass in his hand while he listened to the music. Where would I ever find someone who loved music this deeply? He looked up, saw me watching him, and smiled self-consciously. It was a look I knew well; his lips pursed just a faint smile as his eyes blinked a gentle acknowledgment that he was in tune with me.

I indicated the portrait with my head.

"Claire?"

"*Oui, oui,*" he said casually, "a friend of hers painted it."

I refused to believe that I was in a couple's apartment. In my mind, Luc wasn't really married. After all, Claire wasn't even living in Paris, and when she came back for her fellowships at various hospitals, they slept separately—in two sad little bedrooms. Where were the son's toys, or art supplies, or books? And where did he even sleep? I knew the boy was currently at Claire's parents' in Normandy, but didn't he ever live with his parents? There was not a single indication that a three year old existed, or of a shared family life. By all appearances it looked like an apartment of two remote roommates who were just starting their careers and were never home. But when I furtively opened the medicine cabinet in the bathroom, and saw eye liner and lipstick tucked beneath odd aspirin discs, I couldn't stay deluded for long.

Luc chose records specifically for me. We brought the plates into the kitchen and returned to the living room. I was on the couch. He sat down on the chair. Sensuality and cuddliness didn't come naturally to him.

"Why are you sitting so far away?" I asked gently.

"You want me to come sit there with you?" His formality was astounding, but endearing.

He got up to come sit beside me, and I leaned back against his chest while he put his arms around me. I felt safe and happy in a way that I wasn't used to—calm, understood, loved, and sharing what I cared most about. We turned off the lamp and listened to the music, savoring the ambience in the flickering candlelight.

"Just a second," he said, "don't move. I have one more piece to play for you." He got up and looked for a record in his cabinet, slid it out of its jacket and onto the turntable, carefully putting the needle down on the second track. It was the *Andante*[10] movement from the Schubert B-flat Piano Trio that I had given him, the one I passed through my open window when he came by for the first time.

He came back to me on the couch, easing my shoulders to lean back against his chest, as we both stretched out the length of the couch. We listened together for a long time without a thought about what would come next. I needed more instants like this in my life, when my mind stopped moving forward or backward, and there was only the pleasure of the present moment. He slid his hands under my sweater and rested them on the thin satin of my camisole. With indiscernible small movements he began to move his thumbs lightly over my nipples. My pulse quickened but I let him continue caressing the nubs of flesh without letting on how aroused I was becoming. But my chest began to rise and fall more noticeably, and my breathing quickened. When I couldn't wait any longer, I turned around to face him, straddling his body. My lips only barely brushed his lips at first, teasing their fullness and rose-petal softness. Finally I leaned in and kissed him deeply, swimming dizzily into his body.

Months had passed since we knew we were in love. There would be no more waiting. As we undressed each other timidly, Luc never assumed the role of the older, more experienced lover. He seemed as intimidated as I was, with tentative but poetic caresses, and his gentle discovery of my body as he unfolded my innocence made me want to weep. He seemed desperate not to harm me in any way. I could scarcely believe that this was the same act I had experienced with Miles, in his parents' Connecticut guest room, or with Lefevre, in the back garden of the dilapidated boarding house in Nice. It wasn't about technique, positions or objectives, but about something deeply metaphysical. I was no longer standing at the precipice, but had let go and was flying through the air.

# SEVENTEEN

*Dear Julie,*

*In Paris it is raining, Julie, but I cannot warm myself like we used to in that poetic little room on rue Bonaparte. I remembered last night while listening to the flute in Brahms' Fourth, that when I arrived at your new home in the 6ième, I loved more than anything to hear your flute while I climbed the narrow stairs to your tiny maid's room. I'd be as quiet as possible and would wait in your hallway, delighted to surprise you when I opened the door, the key still in the lock.*

*Luc*

Madame Cammas appeared in the doorway of my room a few weeks later.

"YOU HAVE TO FIND ANOTHER ROOM," she bellowed in her wobbly voice.

"May I ask you why?" I asked innocently, knowing perfectly well that she must have heard Luc's voice in my room recently and concluded that he had been coming in through my window.

"I NEED THE ROOM FOR MY DAUGHTER," she lied.

I was indignant at first, knowing that Madame Cammas was making this up. But soon I felt thankful that my landlady had given me an excuse to move out. Why hadn't I thought of it before? I wouldn't miss her smelly soups, ripe cheeses, and ever-present French *télé* in the background. I wouldn't miss hearing the old woman unlock the front door after running errands, and jingle noisily with her keys as she shuffled down the hall. And I wouldn't miss creeping in softly at night, turning the hefty key, and anticipating her judgmental glare as she stood in the entrance of her living room.

When I told Luc that Madame Cammas was throwing me out, he suggested we scare her a bit by having Philippe call her as my attorney to make sure she returned my deposit. I knew this was unnecessary and mean-spirited, but ever since my arrival in the fall, I had so often felt like a victim in the face of *petit personnel,* bureaucrats behind desks at the post office, American Embassy, or Police Headquarters, who couldn't be bothered to help me with problems of a lost passport or flute left at a bus stop: "A flute of bread?" they'd asked. "*Quel dommage!* What a pity—she won't be able to play *Papa Noël* this Christmas on her flute!" So often had I been frustrated to tears waiting in line for hours only to be greeted finally by the impenetrable, cold face of a French civil servant shaking her forefinger at me: "*Non, c'est impossible!*" Now having two Frenchmen on my side was simply too hard to resist. I let Philippe call her.

Poor Madame Cammas.

"YOU DIDN'T NEED TO CALL A LAWYER!" she wailed at me the next day. "Of course I will give you back your deposit! *Nom de Dieu!* In the name of God! A lawyer!!!"

Philippe told Luc that Madame Cammas had complained to him, "She has *boys* in her room, and what's more, she *hides* it from me!" Luc and he had a good laugh over this, and I felt a bit flattered that I was important enough for Luc to share this episode with his best friend.

So I left Montparnasse and moved into a very inexpensive *chambre de bonne,* a tiny former maid's room on the top floor of an apartment building on rue Bonaparte, in the sixth *arrondissement.* The rent was 100 francs a month, the equivalent of less than twenty-five or thirty dollars at the time. Although the room itself was sparse and rather shabby, there was no more desirable neighborhood on the Left Bank. My building, tucked in among the art galleries and antique stores, was a block from the beautiful, cobbled square, Saint-Germain-des-Prés. The École Nationale des Beaux-Arts was right down the street, and art students were at every corner carrying cumbersome black portfolios under their arms. Storefront windows were plastered with gallery exhibit posters, each one so stunning that I often asked the shop owners for old ones they were taking down so that I could tape them to my walls. Though my building was not grandiose, I felt safe punching in a code to release the sturdy green outer door of the small courtyard before reaching the entrance. Once inside, the red carpeted stairway and wooden railing curved around and around for five flights. On the fifth floor they stopped. There, behind an almost hidden, low door in the wall, a narrow staircase continued up steeply, leading to two tiny attic rooms, the former servants' quarters.

My room had no furniture aside from a scruffy bed, tucked under the eaves, and a threadbare chest of drawers. I had no kitchen and shared a bathroom with an art student down the hall. The small antique oval table migrated to the sixth *arrondissement* with me, and when I carried it up the six flights of stairs and placed it by the tiny square window, it lent a disparate corner of elegance. I filled empty straw-covered Chianti bottles with candles and flowers and taped Bonnard and Vuillard prints over my bed. My faithful radio transmitted *France Musique's* countless direct transmissions of classical concerts from all over Europe into my tiny room.

From my little window I could hear the concierge sweeping the courtyard below, bellowing in Portuguese to her husband and children. But from that same window, I could see the rooftops of Paris and, in the distance, the Pont Royal and a small portion of the Louvre. When it rained, the sound on the zinc roof overhead was mesmerizing and poetic. I was free finally, and in my haven beneath the eaves, I was where I wanted to be.

Now that Luc and I had privacy, I seldom went back to the apartment he shared with Claire, although she was still rarely there. Luc knew the code to the outer courtyard of 8, rue Bonaparte, and could let himself in unannounced. At five-thirty or so when I expected him to be walking up the six flights to my room, I would play my most moving flute pieces, knowing he would linger outside my room to listen secretly for a minute before tapping on my door.

I knew what my playing meant to him. Even though he had chosen law over music, I sensed his palpable awe and envy of my relationship to this cylinder of silver that I held against my lips and blew air through from deep inside my lungs. Sometimes he asked me to explain technical concepts to him, and I was only too happy to oblige. There was something innately sensuous about how to make a full, vibrant sound on the flute by holding one's lips a certain way, wrapping them around a stream of air to change the tone color from intense and dark to cool and hollow. I knew he waited and listened from behind the door because he never knocked until I had paused or finished a movement. When the door opened, my heart leapt.

He always looked out of place in his suit and tie as he ducked his head to come through the low doorway of my modest dwelling. He would beg me not to speak English right away, pleading that he needed time to unwind after a hard day. "Not today . . . *please!*"

"We can go slowly," I would say, always insisting that we maintain our pretext of English lessons—*text as pretext,* I thought. One day, I took a thick, blue-gray, frayed cloth book off the single shelf that was built into the eaves at the foot of my bed. It was another book I had sent over in a box from the States. I suggested we read together calmly from the same book, as I settled into a side-lying position with the book in front of me, inviting him to lie down behind me. Studying was suddenly more appealing to him, and he reluctantly agreed as he kicked off his shoes.

"This is another book I brought from home that I haven't shown you yet," I said. "The English Romantic poets. Have you ever heard of any of these guys? Wordsworth, Coleridge?"

"*Oui, oui* . . . maybe . . . I'm not sure," he answered. "Do you think we'll really get anything done this way?" he asked, already giving me little kisses on the back of my neck.

"Absolutely," I answered, pretending not to notice. "You *need* to learn English," I said with false gravity, "and I see no reason not to be comfortable while we work. I don't want to sit on some hard little café chairs to read English poetry."

I lay on my left side, head propped up by my left arm, and Luc spooned me with his hand on my waist. He looked over my shoulder at the book, opened to one of my favorite Wordsworth poems, *Tintern Abbey*—a lyrical meditation on memory. I loved this poem, and knew many of the lines by heart:

> *And now, with gleams of half-extinguished thought,*
> *With many recognitions dim and faint,*
> *And somewhat of a sad perplexity,*
> *The picture of the mind revives again:*
> *While here I stand, not only with the sense*
> *Of present pleasure, but with pleasing thoughts*
> *That in this moment there is life and food*
> *For future years.*

I knew this poetry was so much more complex and nuanced than the Oscar Wilde fairy tales, but I wanted him to hear its music and flow, even if he couldn't fully grasp its meaning.

He started to read from the beginning, and I corrected each of Luc's words, reminding him often to aspirate the *"h,"* and to put his tongue between his teeth for *"th."* He was sensitive about his dreadful accent, so I assured him that he was doing fine. But the more I felt his warm breath in my ear as he leaned over my shoulder to read, the more I let him get by with not just words, but entire phrases that were completely unintelligible. My legs and arms were covered in goosebumps and after a few more lines, I no longer heard a thing, as I nodded yes with my eyes closed.

*"Mademoiselle Scolnik,"* he said as he kissed the back of my earlobe, "you are not finding any more words to correct?" he asked. And then he rolled me onto my back and kissed me slowly.

"This is . . . of course . . . all . . . in the name . . . of learning . . . all part of the lesson plan," I'd say in bits and pieces when I could get enough air in between kisses. "The lips must be retrained."

In a lazy, lust-filled stupor, burying his face in my neck and hair, he said, "I find that your pedagogical skills are much improved, *Mademoiselle Scolnik*, and very effective. These must be the *nouvelles méthodes d'Anglais.*" The *new* English lessons.

An hour later I walked Luc to the bus stop.

"English lesson tomorrow, Julie?" he asked as his bus drew near.

"New methods or old?" I asked. He smiled and hopped onto the bus, stood in the doorway and waved goodbye as it pulled away. I walked around *Boulevard Saint-Germain* as daylight faded and streets became animated with people heading home to their families, briefcases and baguettes under their arms. I picked up something for dinner from a small market and wandered home slowly.

I didn't mind that Luc left me alone. I felt flush with love as I climbed the five curving flights of stairs, and one steep narrow one to my Lilliputian living quarters at the top. Collapsing on my low bed to read *Madame Bovary*, and listen to my radio, I felt safe and happy. I didn't care about Hemingway, F. Scott Fitzgerald, Gertrude Stein, or any of the dozens of writers who had described the magic of this city. This was *my* Paris now.

# EIGHTEEN

Dear Julie,

Last weekend I spoke in that enormous hall, Salle Bleue, at the Palais des Congrès, where we sang so many concerts together. You inhabited those walls, Julie, and I had the impression that you were amongst the hundreds of lawyers there to hear me. I found myself surprised to speak only to you.

How can I find the words to express this thought, that everything I do, everything I say, everything I am, is probably for the first time in my life received, felt, and heard by you across the world? You have given me, Julie, the taste of a new language and I believe that you will forever be present in everything I have to say.

I waited and listened, hoping that the phone would ring in my office at eleven o'clock this morning as it always did when you called me from a café.

*Luc*

My 11 o'clock calls to Luc's office continued, but now, in my new neighborhood, I had more upscale cafés to make them from. I felt like a regular at Café de Flore, or Café Bonaparte, where neighborhood locals still congregated on the terraces to meet their friends or stood at the zinc bar with their espresso or glass of *rouge*. Deux Magots was a magnificent café across from the church in the square, another iconic meeting place of literati in the fifties. I would regularly make my way to the back of the mosaic-floored interior, stopping first at the bar to order an espresso to earn the right to use the phone. Underneath the *Toilettes/Téléphone* sign in the corner was a narrow, marble, spiral staircase leading to the basement, where I would put a franc in the fat, odd-shaped telephone, and dial Luc's office number. His secretary would pick up.

"*Allô, oui?*"

"Hello, may I please speak to Monsieur Berthelot?"

"*Ne quittez pas.* Just a minute please."

Every few weeks I tried to call home, but it involved a tedious process of putting in a request at a post office, then waiting for thirty minutes until the connection was made. My name and the city of Lewiston, Maine, would be called out in such a strong French accent that I barely recognized it: "*SCOLNEEEK -LEVISTONNE—Cabine Deux!* I would enter a tiny phone booth and try to tell my parents about my new life in Paris.

My lessons with Lefevre had continued with regularity throughout the year. Although I still sometimes regretted that I hadn't enrolled at the Paris Conservatory, I began getting a few referrals of flute jobs with small ensembles through a Danish flutist I knew from Nice. It felt good to be earning money as a flutist in Paris, and helped alleviate my disappointment about my private lessons which had become colorless and uninspiring.

I never told Luc about the incident with Lefevre that summer in Nice. But he seemed to sense intuitively that there was some history between us. As Lefevre was a well-regarded flutist in France, Luc asked if he could sit in on one of my lessons, and I cautiously agreed.

I suspected that meeting my older, French lawyer boyfriend might intimidate Lefevre on many levels, as he would no longer be able to attribute my rejection of him to my inexperience or puritanical American mores.

Sure enough, the hour was intensely uncomfortable for all three of us, and degenerated further when the discussion turned to the Orchestre de Paris and Lefevre made an anti-Semitic remark about Daniel Barenboim—that he had invited all his little Jewish friends to conduct the orchestra (and he was talking about Zubin Mehta, who is Indian, not Israeli). Luc could not stay silent at this, and put Lefevre in his place with a subtle but condescending retort.

On the way home, Luc admitted that he hated Lefevre for his petty, racist views. He hated him for having known me longer than he had, and for reasons he could not explain. At my next lesson, Lefevre was bad-tempered, and seemed to communicate his humiliation by falsely accusing me of forgetting to pay him the week before.

As we got to know each other better, I learned that it bothered Luc to see me interacting with men as freely as I did. In fact, many of the waiters in my favorite cafés knew my name, and one had asked me out once. I didn't accept, but I was neither rude nor offended. My relationship with them quickly changed once Luc came into the picture, as they no longer spoke easily with me when he was around. I thought of these waiters as my friends, and wasn't aware that my behavior was inappropriate, but Luc called me on it once he felt comfortable enough to bring it up. He used himself as an example, explaining that he had had so many *'incidents'* in his life that he had learned to be very careful not to lead women on. Then, as if he had been working up to this, he said, "*Toi*, you are not careful enough."

I was used to hearing that I was too flirtatious; I had heard it for so many years that it was old, tedious news. But I didn't agree with the notion and had endless ways to explain why. So I gave it a shot.

"I don't agree with you," I began. "It's just my personality, how I relate to the world. You cannot call it flirting when I act exactly the same way with women and children! I could no sooner change how I act with people than I could change my height or the color of my eyes. Besides, even if men think I am being flirtatious, they soon learn that I act this way with everyone. I always assume their intentions are innocent," I said.

"Julie," he said, as if it were the most obvious thing in the world, "but *of course* people have intentions. *I* have intentions. I have very serious intentions being here."

I smiled. Although I found him patronizing, it touched me that he cared enough to bring it up, that he wanted me for himself. For the first time ever, I started to reconsider my behavior. Besides, I had already begun to smile less often at strangers ever since an elderly lady turned to me as we waited to cross a street, and said kindly, "You are not French, *n'est-ce pas, mademoiselle?* French people don't smile like that at each other." I decided that I would try to be more careful. It was probably time to grow up. After that moment, I consciously tried to tone down my ebullience in everyday encounters with people.

If we weren't trying to study English, late afternoon hours with Luc were spent playing with each other and going over old memories from the beginning of our courtship. One afternoon we lay on the bed, my head nestled in the nook of his chest and shoulder, rising and falling with his calm breathing. As he caressed my cheek, tucking little wisps of hair behind my ear, we talked about those eight days when we first met and sat side by side for three consecutive Beethoven concerts, when the Ninth Symphony had become what Proust had described as the *"National Hymn of our love."*

It was sweet to compare memories, to hear from him things I had only imagined—namely his first impressions of me.

"That first night," he said, "when you came up to me, and tapped me on the shoulder, I listened to nothing you said, but watched your hands in motion, your darting eyes, and especially your eyebrows. In five minutes I sensed a great deal about you."

"Like what?" I asked, dreading his answer.

"Oh, many psychological things," he teased. "At first I thought you must be very bold to approach me like that, but then I noticed that you avoided my eyes, and when I drove you home, you grabbed for the door handle before the car had even stopped."

I briefly considered this assessment.

"Hmm," I began, "I guess that's fair. But, I noticed a lot of things about you, too! Do you have any idea how you came across?" I asked. "You were so cold. You walked two paces ahead of me all the way to your car that first night, as if you wanted to make sure it could not possibly have been construed as interest." I paused. "A few nights later, though, you turned off the car motor when we got to my building."

"*Ça m'énerve!*" he replied. "It annoys me that you noticed that!"

Luc reminded me that I deliberately waited until 11:30 to call him that first time when he asked me to call at 11, and that I walked past him at the chorus to talk to someone without acknowledging him. He reproached me for playing such games.

"Listen," I challenged him. "Remember how you acted when I kissed you good night those first nights. You gave me no choice but to retreat. I thought the *bise* was a cultural thing, that it was universal, like a handshake. But I understood immediately by your reaction that I was wrong."

"Yes," he agreed. "I don't kiss people indiscriminately. It is not in my nature."

I felt embarrassed as I thought back to all those times I flaunted a double goodbye kiss with Dominique in front of Luc. We talked about the difference between the French *tu* and *vous,* the familiar and formal forms of "you."

"I 'tutoyer' everyone," I said casually. "I know it's very American, but I don't see the point in making the distinction, and I know I can get away with it."

"I disagree entirely with your attitude," Luc stated. "I appreciate very much choosing *vous* with one secretary, for instance, and *tu* with another. And it's a very nice moment when one changes to *tu* in a friendship."

*Merde.* And he still wasn't finished.

"To hear you use *tu* that first night when you tapped me on the shoulder was somewhat shocking, but I had no choice except to use it back with you. Did you notice how long it took me before I even *knew* your first name, never mind called you by it, whereas you were throwing '*Luc*' into the conversation every two minutes!"

*Okay, okay, I get it.*

"But Julie, you know what really made me look at you for the first time?"

"What?"

"The night when we stopped for a drink with Dominique after a rehearsal. And you offered me your tea."

I instantly remembered that post-rehearsal drink in the café, the night when Luc asked me about finding an English teacher, and we completely ignored Dominique.

He continued. "You may think this ridiculous or exaggerated, but I was touched by your gesture because there is something intimate, symbolic . . . mythological, even, about drinking from the same cup. I had just finished an icy cold beer. The last thing in the world I wanted was hot tea," he said.

"Why did you accept it then?"

"There was no way I could turn you down."

Half-heartedly putting his jacket back on, he swept his hair back with one hand and stood up. He was leaving me again. It was always seven or seven-thirty when he sighed and stood up. Even when Claire was not living in Paris, he never digressed from this time table. Was it to maintain appearances, or maybe to be available in case she called? I never asked him to stay longer or asked why he couldn't. There was always the next day to look forward to—an English lesson in a café or park, a chorus rehearsal in the evening, or a late afternoon tryst on rue Bonaparte. Before we said goodbye each night, Luc often checked the radio schedule in *Le Monde* to see if there was a live broadcast that we could listen to simultaneously, connected through the airwaves.

On the days when he couldn't come by my room after work, he often asked me to meet him near his office on a small street off the Champs-Elysées, rue Lincoln. Time was an extravagance I had that spring, and I was only too delighted to flash my *carte orange* to the driver of bus No. 39 or No. 95, and head toward the Right Bank. I would sit by an open window and savor the ride across the bridge to Place de la Concorde, then four stops up the Champs-Elysées to his office on rue Lincoln. A café on the corner knew me well, and I would walk downstairs to the public telephone, and call Luc to say that I had arrived.

"*Bonjour, Luc, je suis en bas*. I am downstairs at The Red Lion."

I continued to be dumbstruck that a naïve twenty-year-old American girl, oblivious to haute couture, haute cuisine, current events, and countless other things that the French held dear, could pull this important lawyer out of a meeting to the telephone, and to an afternoon rendezvous. That he desired my company over so many more sophisticated, fashionable, and intellectual French women in his circle was a constant source of bewilderment to me.

# NINETEEN

---

*Dear Julie,*

*It is 5:30. You called me three hours ago and I am still lost. You cannot imagine how much I wanted to hold you and to speak to you softly. This sad and desperate tone in your voice worries me so much. It's so complex for me that in one second, I leave my ridiculous lawyer's face to escape and hear your voice. Suddenly we create our own universe, our own territory, which will never exist with anyone else. This is new for me.*

*Julie, don't despair, we'll find a solution to these problems with the Administration. I am still confidant that I will be sent to work in the USA soon. Don't let yourself feel overwhelmed by the people around you. You are more vulnerable and fragile than you realize. Preserve yourself for the things which are worthy of your enormous wealth of talent—tenderness, love, music, intelligence, poetry.*

*Your call was a gift today. Thank you.*

*Luc*

"I expect that Claire will leave me anyway, once she learns that I am in love with someone else," he said to me as we walked across Pont Neuf sharing an umbrella one drizzly day. The deep green hues of the trees hung low over the Seine, and Paris in the rain looked sad and poetic, as only it could. We stopped and leaned against the railings, looking down at the river.

"But wouldn't you end it anyway on your own?" I tried to understand.

"It's not that simple," he said. "I want to see if my relationship with you deepens first."

I paused. "What do you mean? If it doesn't, you would just stay married?"

"But no, that's not it. It's just not the time to have a big marital flare-up in the midst of this fragile time in Claire's medical studies. Remember what I told you. This is not an emotionally stable woman we're talking about. We have spoken of a separation happening in June, when she completes her medical degree, and begins her career as a doctor. We only stayed together out of financial and logistical convenience. And divorce is also complicated in France when a woman has had serious instability issues."

It was deeply disturbing to hear him speak of her as unstable. How unstable was she? Even though he had shared a bit with me about her emotional frailty, I couldn't bear to process what role this might play in our story.

"But I finally got very good news today," he continued, as we left the bridge and continued to stroll along the *quais* by the booksellers. "It looks as if I am going to be sent to the U.S. for certain to work for at least six months. It will facilitate the end of my marriage, and avoid a direct confrontation with Claire, which is what I was counting on all along," he explained.

Then my stomach knotted, and suddenly I knew. I stopped on the sidewalk to look at him and asked: "Does Claire ever *try* to get close to you?"

He answered with a small, resigned, "She tries."

Aha. That changed everything. So it wasn't as simple as he had implied. In fact, Claire was probably very attached to him. I told him this.

"No, she isn't, really. As far as she's concerned, she'd rather be with me than alone. I don't say this conceitedly, but even though she doesn't want to be with me, she tells me that she probably can't find anyone better. She likes bringing me to events where I can be charming and witty, that's all. But we have nothing in common, except on a certain intellectual level. Mostly, my presence seems to annoy her. She often storms into the living room where I am listening to music and turns it off without asking me, saying that it's too loud or is giving her a headache. We fight about stupid things—whose turn it was to buy groceries, for instance, or clean the kitchen. And we never talk about or share anything important. So many times she has told me that she will be gone when I get home, but she never leaves, or leaves and then returns in tears, unable to do it."

I listened attentively to these explanations. I didn't know they shared groceries. Just how estranged were they, exactly? I often shook my head in disbelief. From all outward appearances I was living an embarrassing cliché, in love with a married man.

As we turned down rue Bonaparte from the Seine, past small art galleries and *tabacs*, it started to rain harder, and we had to run the last block to escape a downpour. Once we reached my room, the sound of the rain on the zinc roof above was as steady and rhythmic as a snare drum. We dried off and lay down under the eaves. Luc had one arm bent under his head as he lay on his back. I had untucked his button-down shirt and was stroking his stomach. I lay on my side propped up on one arm.

"Why are there initials on your pocket?" I asked. "L.B."

"Oh that," he answered sheepishly. "As *fonctionnaire,* a civil servant, I am given these shirts by the government," he said. "This job," he continued quietly, "is the biggest contradiction in my life.

"After the Sorbonne and law school, I had to undergo a rigorous application process to get accepted into L'ÉNA, the administrative school. The candidates had to sit facing a semicircle of panelists who fired questions at us in front of a live audience. At the start of my interview, one of the older women on the jury said to me, 'So you are interested in administration, *monsieur?*'

'Am I not here for that, madame?' I answered.

'With your looks I am surprised that you are not in the cinema,' she continued, not to flatter me, but rather to throw me off, derail me.

'Madame, with your looks, I am not at all surprised that you are a bureaucrat,' I answered, while my friends in the audience could scarcely control themselves."

He enjoyed telling stories that demonstrated his scathing wit. But I didn't need more evidence of these attributes. Besides, as much as his face could move me when he was being sensitive and considerate, a certain arrogant smile altered Luc's face when he was enjoying his own sarcasm. Oddly enough, this particular look reminded me of the grinning flying monkeys in *The Wizard of Oz*. I was just glad not to be on the receiving end of his ridicule.

It frustrated me that I hadn't been able to share my innate, domestic side with Luc. So one day I decided to cook an elaborate meal for him and bring it to his apartment. I had met a lovely American girl who was enrolled at one of the venerated culinary schools in Paris, and she offered to help me prepare a classic French dish to offer to my beau, even if I had no place for entertaining. One afternoon we shopped and hauled groceries to her apartment on rue de Grenelle, and spent the afternoon in her kitchen making a chicken dish with shallots, wine, and crème fraîche.

Metros and buses were all I knew, and it didn't occur to me to spend money on a taxi. So across the city I journeyed in two buses to transport this meal in a heavy earthenware *Le Creuset* pot from the seventh *arrondissement* all the way to Luc's building in the fourteenth. The luscious aroma of onions, garlic, and wine wafted out of my wicker basket from my seat, while perplexed little old ladies seated nearby stared. When I got off the second bus, I still had several blocks to walk to reach his apartment. I had to keep switching the heavy basket from hand to hand every half block because of its weight, and by the time I arrived, my forearms were aching, and I couldn't uncurl my sore red fingers.

"Did you buy any bread?" is all Luc asked after we had sat down to eat. I had not. Then he continued: "This is the kind of food my parents eat; most people I know now cook what's called *'nouvelle cuisine,'* not as rich, fewer sauces. Simpler cooking."

I wilted. And when we were finished and began cleaning up, although we had eaten less than half of what I made, he said, "I guess we'll have to throw away the rest; Claire comes back tomorrow." I watched as he scraped the remaining chicken pieces with succulent sauce into his garbage bin.

There were other minor hurts. Philippe invited Luc on long sailing trips, and it didn't occur to either one to invite me. I tossed it aside by reminding myself that I was a busy student and couldn't miss classes or lessons, and I felt pleased that Luc never saw me as needy or dependent.

But one day when I called, he asked me to meet near his office for lunch. His voice was tense, and I had never heard him so upset. It seemed that during one of my very infrequent visits to his apartment, a panty liner had gone astray in his bed. Claire found it while doing the laundry. I didn't *know* Claire did their laundry. He seemed to blame me, nearly implying that I had planted it on purpose. I was stung and shocked by his reaction to the whole incident. I was sorry it happened, but I figured that our relationship was bound to be exposed sooner or later, and wasn't that what Luc wanted ultimately? Everything was going to have to be dealt with much sooner than he had planned, he said, as if this were a bad thing.

But he was mistaken. Although Claire confronted him with her discovery, he refused to discuss it, and the subject was dropped. His infidelity was clearly not enough to end their marriage. The fact that Claire was willing to tolerate this level of blatant betrayal was hard for me to fathom, and it implied something significant about how difficult a divorce might be.

In my wanderings around the city, I often felt envious. Envious of couples sitting at intimate, candlelit bistros as I passed them on my way home to eat cross-legged on my bed in my tiny attic room. Envious of the grandiose, luxury hotels such as Hotel de Crillon which I would pass by, momentarily dizzy with desire to enter. I longed to sit in the spacious sitting rooms with seventeenth century tapestries, upholstered arm chairs, and mahogany writing desks. Sometimes, when I thought I looked presentable, I would saunter through the lobby of one of them, pretend to be a guest, and sit down on one of the plush couches to read or write a letter. But I never fooled anyone, and after a single inquiry from a hotel staff member—"How can we help you, *Mademoiselle*?"—I would flee with shame.

I wanted to explain to them that I was comfortable in this milieu, that as a child I spent every school vacation in my grandfather's hotel in Washington, D.C. Political parties, with sumptuous banquets of Russian specialty dishes, were held often in the hotel dining room, and my sisters and I felt important in our velvet party dresses and black patent leather Mary Jane shoes, dancing in the arms of our grandfather to the Russian tunes of the accordion player. Like many others of his time, my grandfather had come to this country from the villages and shtetels of Eastern Europe with no money, no English, and no help from others. He peddled ties, apples, and sheets on the streets of the lower East Side until he was able to buy a clothing store in Washington. Two stores later, he bought an apartment building across from the National Cathedral which he gradually converted into a hotel that catered to diplomatic personnel who worked on Embassy Row.

The lobby of the Alban Towers Hotel was an immense magical playground for me and my sisters during our childhood visits. In our games of hide and seek we found extraordinary hiding places behind the thick velvet drapes in the lobby, under piles of shirts in dry cleaner bins, behind the counter of the drugstore's soda fountain, and in the endless echo-y stairwells. The smiling hotel personnel allowed special privileges to Mr. Revitz's three granddaughters who floated freely through its floors. This is why I was so disappointed to last only seconds in one of the Paris hotels, whose staff saw right through my pretense that I belonged.

Sometimes my disquietude about being with a married man would surface in my dreams. Once as I drifted into sleep, the air was filled with the eerie and foreboding *"Dies Irae"* theme from Berlioz's *Symphonie Fantastique*. The funeral bells announcing the Day of Wrath resounded all around me, as if carried by the wind. I awoke in my dark room feeling alone and panicky.

Then one day when I was out and about in my Saint-Germain neighborhood, I ran into an old Exeter classmate. Warren was a tall, broad-shouldered rower one year ahead of me at Exeter, and besides finding him sultry and handsome, I had admired his sensitive submissions in the school literary magazine. At his early graduation in January, I bravely confessed that I had noticed him from afar, throwing caution to the wind, as I believed that he was about to leave the school permanently. He told me he was *not* leaving, in fact, but staying on as a post-grad for the second semester. My declaration, though mortifying, was inconsequential, as he had a serious girlfriend at Exeter anyway. After that day, we would wave to each other from a distance, and smile when we passed in the dining hall.

When I saw him serendipitously in my Paris neighborhood, he told me he was spending the year studying there, too, and was clearly unattached now. Although I found him just as appealing, and the attraction seemed to be mutual, I avoided him categorically because of Luc, even refusing to get coffee together. I later called him from a café to explain my bizarre behavior.

Yet even with intermittent loneliness, random insensitivity from Luc, and the subtle disorientation of seeing Warren, I had never felt this happy in my life. I saw a difficult road ahead, but trusted Luc to find a way. The small things that concerned me about him were immaterial next to the qualities that convinced me I had met my kindred soul. There was a quiet undercurrent of awe that we had found each other. There would be no other love in my life, I was sure of it.

"I'm ruining you, somewhat," Luc said one day under my eaves. "I'm so afraid of upsetting your equilibrium. You are way too young to be entering into this mess."

*Too late.*

"I've already lived through such an enormous personal failure in my life, with my marriage," he continued. "If I were to cause you any hurt or disappointment, I wouldn't be able to stand it."

*Too late.*

"Still," he added in a soft voice as he touched my face with the back of his hand, "it's not too sad to know that someone loves you, is it?

He stood up to leave.

"Oh, wait just a moment," he added, as he was walking out the door.

"I wrote something for you last night when I was alone in my apartment."

He reached into his inner jacket pocket and pulled out a folded piece of paper, then leaned down to kiss me goodbye. When I could no longer hear him walking down the narrow stairs outside my door, I unfolded the note he had handed me, written in dull blue pencil:

*Moonlight floods my room where I imagine you lying in wait for me, but in spite of these memories, there is only darkness now. How can I forget those moments at dusk when the world outside your window became but shadows and your eyes lit up suddenly with wild mischief? Knowing your laughter has brought me to life, Julie. That one night you will leave me, all these hours will have been but a single instant.*

*These lips that you played against mine like a feather will obsess me until I can once again feel their soft touch. When I awoke, chilled and trembling from a bad dream, I felt my fever disappear through your whispers. I am vulnerable. I saw it in your eyes as your hair flowed down over your shoulders like a downpour of rain.*

*So there you have it Julie, some words which I cannot whisper into your ear tonight, in the darkness of my bedroom, in a low voice, when everything becomes tenderness, when you would help ease me into sleep.*

# TWENTY

Dear Julie,

*I am going to try to make you feel what I felt during the first rehearsal after summer break. Imagine. Everything was like it was three months ago in June before you left. You know, I haven't told anyone that you have left Paris, because I like seeing your name on the attendance sheet. I have the impression that you are just late and will be arriving soon. There were no more looks to each other from afar and I returned to my solitude. Each passage of Brahms Requiem where we glanced at each other (because it was too beautiful), sends me to your smile, your look, to you. Of course I am dying to be with you, but beyond that, I cannot imagine singing this music without you. It's a true scandal.*

*This stunning memory in the sun,*
*The forests of Fontainebleau were silenced when you left,*
*Each leaf wilted.*
*One kiss, one more kiss, just one,*
*To no longer think of the desert*

Spring was late in coming to Paris that year, with rain and drizzle falling relentlessly through late April and early May. I had left most of my school essays until the last minute, so I remained cloistered for hours in my little *Bohème*-like garret, writing French papers by hand on crinkly onion skin paper, while listening to the sound of the rain on my roof above.

Miraculously, it seemed that as soon as my last paper had been delivered, the sun came out, and Paris exploded into a wild profusion of colors and scents. Parks and gardens flourished. Street vendors on rue de Seine built pyramids of peaches and strawberries, and smiling Parisians filled every table at sun-drenched cafés.

Luc and I were grateful that our chorus rehearsals continued throughout the month of June. The Thursday and Friday evenings became stolen, legitimate hours we could spend together. We were beginning the sumptuous Brahms Requiem, a brand new discovery for me. I was disappointed, though, that I would miss the performances in the fall, long after I had gone back to the States.

Just days before my flight back home, Luc and I went to FNAC to buy a record of *Les Petits Chanteurs à la Croix de Bois*, for me to take home to the States. He helped me choose one in which he sang all of the solos. On the front of the record jacket was a photo of the choir standing in front of the stained-glass windows of Sainte-Chapelle and this passage:

> *The most celebrated children's choir in the world, over 10,000 concerts in 65 countries. Thank you, Petits Chanteurs, for this breath of fresh air, this message of beauty, friendship, and love.*

Inside the jacket cover there were three photos from their tours. In all of them, the little boys stood in two straight lines next to the priests. In the Louvre they were each clad in a long white robe. In the others, standing before the Eiffel Tower, and in front of an immense statue of Buddha in the Far East, the little boys wore short trousers, white knee socks, and black V-neck sweaters. Luc drew an *X* on the tiniest boy in the middle of the front row.

Even though I could have applied for grants to allow me to remain in Paris as a music student, I made a deliberate decision not to. I felt that staying there implied an unspoken acceptance of our limited relationship—the short windows of time in which we could meet, the late-afternoon goodbyes. I thought it best to follow through with my original plan to return home and finish my senior year at Wesleyan. I hoped that the pain of separation would jolt Luc into realizing that he would have to do something about his life and become a free man. And, of course, if that were to happen, I might very well be on the next plane back to Paris.

Luc tried to spend as much time as possible with me during my remaining days. We took special trips in the late afternoons to Parc Monceau and Versailles. The day before my flight home, we spent the afternoon at Fontainebleau. The sun was strong on my newly bared shoulders, and the air smelled like fresh earth and flower blossoms as we wandered the sculpted gardens. We walked through the acres of woodland that adjoined the chateau, estranged by our sorrow and inability to talk about the future. Luc saw my face and tried to reach me.

"Julie. I am living in a remarkably changing period of my life now," he said as we found a bench in the sun. "On *every* level," he continued. "My seven years of working for the administration are coming to an end, so I don't know what lies ahead for me professionally. Meeting you took me totally by surprise. It is not in my character to make false promises, to talk of our future happiness. I don't *have* the answers. Just know that in two minutes I would hop on a plane to the U.S. to help you with a philosophy paper like I did for you last week on Dialectic Thought in your little maid's room."

It was enough for me.

On June 26, after everything in my room had been packed or thrown away, only a profusion of dried flowers remained. Yellow daffodils that had become dark gold and were curling around the necks of Chianti bottles, and pink roses which had dried into a deep fuchsia were mixed in with vases of purple statice. I just couldn't throw them into the trash.

"You know what you should do?" Luc proposed. "You should throw your flowers into the Seine."

My face lit up, as I imagined these flowers—tangible memories of our months together in that little maid's room—floating down the Seine. Luc pulled his small car up onto the sidewalk in front of 8 rue Bonaparte, and carried my suitcase and flute bag down the six flights. I used all my fingers to gather up my dried flowers, careful not to crush them. My pinky scooped up the tiniest curled stem of a rose I had pinned over my bed under the eaves; this one had assumed a face and soul with its barely opened petals resembling pouty lips.

I ran down the six flights of stairs, and Luc opened the car door for me as I carefully got into his little purring VW. We drove the car to the closest bridge, Pont des Arts, abandoned it at an illegal spot on the *quai,* and ran to the black iron railings. Peering over the edge at the dizzying sight, I let go of both fistfuls at once, as Luc and I watched the gold, purple, and pink confetti petals fly through the air and land in a clump in the swirling waters. The flowers floated under the bridge, so we ran quickly to the other side to watch them become smaller and smaller, and finally disappear from sight.

"They'll go all the way to the sea," Luc said.

Neither one of us could speak in the car as we drove to the airport. The same neighborhoods that I had grown to know and love so intimately sped by me now as I looked out my passenger window. My throat had an aching lump from trying not to cry. When we got out of his car, I saw that it was best to leave quickly. The blood had drained from Luc's face and I had never witnessed such a visceral disintegration of spirit. We embraced slowly, and I rested my cheek against his chest. His heart was beating fast and his breathing had quickened. He kissed the top of my head, and told me it was going to be ok. Our bodies tore apart at the TWA escalator, and Luc turned away quickly. I rode the moving stairs up without turning around, as if, like Lot's wife, I might turn to salt if I did.

# Part Two

# TWENTY-ONE

———— ⤳✦⤳ ————

WHEN I RETURNED TO MY parents' house in Maine at the end of June, I was not the same girl who had left nine months earlier. It wasn't just the French words I was throwing unwittingly into all my conversations or the entertaining stories I recounted about Madame Cammas, losing my passport, leaving my flute at a bus stop, or the transformative concerts I sang under Daniel Barenboim. It wasn't the new sophistication of my strappy, high-heeled sandals or the brown smudgy Kohl eyeliner that I now wore under my bottom eyelashes. What my parents saw most clearly was that their youngest daughter was in love.

Five days later I received what would be the first of hundreds of letters from Luc. It was written in minute handwriting on light airmail paper and folded into an almost square rectangle. For the rest of the summer, when not practicing or working part-time in a local bookstore, I was writing long letters to him, and living day to day waiting for his to arrive. These letters revealed a sensitive side that he hid from the world, and they made me love him more. Every day I would walk down Mountain Avenue towards Bates College from my parents' house to intercept the mailman, unable to wait a minute longer than I had to.

*Paris. June 1977*

*Dear Julie,*

*This letter won't reach you for days. When it does, I hope that you will have regained your equilibrium. As for me, I am sinking like a ship in a storm.*

*Yesterday, after you left, I lived through one of the most difficult days of my life. My body was knotted up, as if when your plane took off, all the anguish that you knew how to appease, surprised me again with even more force, more tenacity.*

*To know that you live with six hours behind me gives me the sensation of always being incapable of any possible communication between us because I cannot calculate my daily acts with yours. To be ahead of this system is depressing; I would prefer to be six hours behind you.*

*Paris seems absurd. Yesterday, so as not to struggle against invincible forces, I drove down both rue Brown-Séquard and rue Bonaparte, hoping you might appear. How can I make you understand my despair with this distance of time and space? Please tell me as much as you can about your life back home. At least you know where I live and work. But I can only try to imagine where you are in this vast unknown, and it's unbearable. This week-end without the English lesson.*

*Luc*

◌◌

My days were consumed poring over sonnets by Shakespeare and Browning, and the early love poetry of William Butler Yeats in order to find better ways to express my feelings: *"I have spread my dreams under your feet/ Tread softly because you tread on my dreams."*

I *was* that sensitive girl Luc thought I was. He may have been the first to really see me. When he explained in his letters that I was able to pierce through the protective shell that he hid behind, that I could unlock him as no one else could, I felt as if I alone held the key to his true nature, the one that others couldn't see.

One time, instead of writing, I made a cassette tape for him, a recorded letter of sorts, with a bittersweet piano work by Liszt called *"Au bord d'une source,"*[11] in the background. I spoke softly in French about how I missed him and what I was doing with my days. When I replayed the tape, I was astonished to be so affected by my own melancholy voice. Loving someone, I remembered Mr. Fielding had told his class, is how people learn to love themselves. "I love you, I love *me*," is what it really meant, he said. Love depended less upon what you saw in a person, he told us, than upon what they made you see in yourself. I did often see myself through Luc's eyes, and I was the truest, best version of myself that I had ever been before.

# TWENTY-TWO

*Dear Julie,*

*I just returned from listening to the tape that you sent me. Tears, in spite of myself, filled my eyes and I couldn't stop myself. You know my reserve, Julie, my embarrassment, at this kind of thing. Imagine my pain before cracking in such a way. I can only tell you I am not worthy of such love, so moving are your words, which touch my deepest being. Know that the sound of your voice in its sadness moved me deeply, and made my eyes fill with tears. Why, Julie, you who are usually so happy, why were you so sad?*

*The Brahms Requiem concert was very affecting, and Barenboim seemed to be full of emotion and grateful to the chorus. It was difficult for me to sing this music without you, but I recorded one of the performances for you from the live broadcast. The ability to be moved by music is tied to the possibility to communicate with someone. I felt your presence while I was singing, and knowing that you'd be hearing our performance helped me stay calm and serene.*

*It will take me some time to digest this cassette that you sent. Why didn't you play the flute for me? I am very sorry that you didn't. Write to me.*

*Luc*

CR

When the two long months of summer were over, I returned to Wesleyan for my final year. Suspended in a fragile emotional state, I arrived at the tree-lined campus with a new look in my eyes. What was I doing here, in this bland Connecticut town, more than three thousand miles away from the man I loved?

My trip to the student post office was the highlight of my day. I went twice, once in the morning, and once in the afternoon, just in case. Through the little glass door of P.O. Box 1234, I'd spot a thin, pale, blue airmail envelope and my heart would race. My fingers would tremble as I slid one under the delicate sealed flap. Spiriting the letter away to a quiet, solitary place, I would imagine Luc's voice and drink in his words. Then I'd tuck the missive into a paperback where I could slide it out easily during class without being seen: *". . . Know that there is someone in the world who thinks of you day after day, like the fire under the ash, secretly, ardently."*

His words stayed with me as I crisscrossed campus paths to my French class, to the music building. And then I'd walk around slightly tipsy, as if a tonic had entered my bloodstream. When I wasn't bicycling to classes or sitting in rehearsals, I was reading his letters, writing back, and day-dreaming on the narrow single bed in my off-campus apartment.

But my letters seemed insufficient to me for the magnitude of my feelings. Since childhood, I had always had a penchant for concocting romantic surprises. French lace cookies, miraculous edible amber lace dotted with teeny pecans, had often been my surprise token of affection to a boy or teacher I liked. I used to press perfect reddish-orange fall leaves or velvety rose petals into thick art books, only to be unearthed later when I needed something to slip in with a poem I wanted to send someone. I would collect small objects of charm regularly when I chanced upon them—an oval eraser imprinted with Saint-Exupéry's *Le Petit Prince;* long, slim bookmarks of a particular Klimt painting from a museum; pounded tiny metal hearts to keep with one's spare change; miniature, three-inch leather editions of complete Shakespeare plays.

This was different, of course. There was only one gift I could imagine for Luc that would encompass the scope of my love: I would knit him a scarf for his birthday in October.

Several trips to the yarn store in my college town left me disappointed with the limited colors and varieties of yarn, so I took a two-hour bus from Wesleyan into Boston where I walked long blocks and scoured stores for a wider selection. For forty minutes I stood in front of the bins of yarns at a store on Boylston Street and considered all the choices—smooth and thin, thick and nubby, in every possible shade. Holding one skein after another against my neck to make sure it wasn't itchy, I finally decided on a soft alpaca which was just the right color—blue-gray—the color of Luc's eyes, and the only color he could see. I delved in right away, casting the first row of stitches onto the needle as I rode the bus back to Connecticut. Knit two, pearl two. Over and over again. Knit two, pearl two, created a stretchy ribbed pattern. I loved the way the long aluminum knitting needles slid against each other, and the tactile pleasure of the yarn between my fingers, as rows of perfectly symmetrical stitches multiplied.

Each day I admired my progress as the scarf grew from inches to feet in a matter of weeks. When I finished it, I scoured the downtown stores of Middletown, Connecticut, for the perfect eight-inch-square white gift box, lined it with tissue paper, and folded the scarf neatly into it like a ribbon of taffy. I sent the package off to Paris just in time for his birthday on October 11.

# TWENTY-THREE

*Dear Julie,*

*I just received a package. You hide so many talents from me! I cannot believe how beautiful this scarf is—I will never take it off!*

*The description that you wrote of your classes and professors gives me the impression of a very busy but pleasant life—all these teachers that you call by their first names! That makes me laugh. (At the Sorbonne nobody calls me Luc!) Your heavy schedule must make you panic a bit after your year in Paris where you seemed to have one class every two days!*

*You will laugh, but I, too, have become a student again! Your letters about your school life seduced me so much that I registered for some English courses at the Sorbonne. It's very funny to find myself among young students who are just beginning their studies. I am like a dinosaur from the old world and the teachers are a bit annoyed by my presence.*

*Julie, you know that I have a hard time talking about my emotions. Just know that your scarf touched me more deeply than you can imagine.*

*Thank you*

*Luc*

CR

At the end of October, the small cinema in the Center for the Arts at Wesleyan was showing *The Umbrellas of Cherbourg*, described by its filmmaker, Jacques Demy, as "a love story which finishes badly." It was a new genre of French film—sung from beginning to end in free verse with gorgeous jazzy tunes by the great songwriter, Michel Legrand. Romantic scenes in cafés abound where Guy tells Geneviève that he must serve his military duty in Algeria, and Geneviève begs him not to leave her. (*I can't live without you, Don't go! I will die, I will hide you and care for you, but my love, don't leave me!*[12]) She tearfully promises to wait for him, and he talks her into creating a memory that will sustain them, as he leads her to his bed. They say a gut-wrenching farewell as Guy boards a train and waves goodbye.

The poignancy of this film was entirely lost on my college community. One by one my classmates made it clear just how absurd they found it by getting up to leave in the middle of a scene, each person trying to make a funnier exit as they stood, unleashing the spring of the green plush movie seat. Perhaps it was the constant singing that annoyed them or the Matisse-like surreal pink and green sets. But when Geneviève places the gold cardboard crown on her head—a centuries-old French celebration of the Epiphany with the traditional *Galette des Rois* cake—that was the final straw for a dozen more people whose chairs released at once, to everyone's great amusement. Streams of students exited the little theatre to find other things to do on their hallowed Saturday night. By the end of the film, virtually every person had left the theater, except for me and the friend I had come with, who told me he was staying only to avoid hurting my feelings. I told him he could leave.

A pregnant Geneviève doesn't wait for Guy in the end, but is urged by her mother to marry a wealthy traveling jeweler. Guy finally returns from the military to learn that she has married and moved away. Six years later Guy and Geneviève run into each other by chance in the snow at a gas station; they exchange a few strained words, and she tells him how much her daughter resembles him, asks if he wants to see her. No, I think you better leave, he says, and she drives away in the snow.

Although the small movie theater had emptied out at least an hour earlier, one college girl sat steadfastly engaged until the bitter end, tears streaming down her cheeks, as the credits rolled, the snow fell, and the love theme modulated a half-step higher one more time.

# TWENTY-FOUR

*Dear Julie,*

*I haven't written in a few days but you will understand why. In December I am coming to New York with Philippe who will trade his first-class ticket in for two in coach, and in exchange, I will help him with some legal meetings in NY that he has scheduled. I cannot sleep any more, so excited am I by this news. I am coming just to see you and it is all thanks to Philippe that this trip is happening. Will we be bothering you during your classes? The only thing is that I cannot spend very much money on hotels, etc. Can you find us somewhere to stay? Will you be able to show me Maine in the snow?*

*Luc*

This was unexpected news! I was elated about the visit, except that it involved Philippe, to whom we were supposed to feel deeply grateful. It was a bit surprising that two grown men, successful lawyers no less, were asking me to lodge them. I tried to be gracious by inviting them both to Wesleyan while I finished my last classes before the Christmas break, and then to my parents' home in Maine before going to New York for their meetings.

Driving to New Haven with a borrowed car in order to meet them was already a stretch for me, as I had barely any experience driving. When I first saw Luc, it was instantly apparent that we were not alone. In front of Philippe, he wasn't the person I knew in private, nor was he uninhibited or secure enough to show me the affection I desperately missed.

Instead of occupying himself for a week while Luc spent time with me at Wesleyan, Philippe tagged along like a chaperone to every class, meal, and rehearsal. It drastically altered the dynamic between us. Luc explained that the law firm had offered to add this extra week onto the New York business trip in order to sweeten the deal for him, but only if it didn't add to the total cost of the trip.

At first it was fun, and I was quietly thrilled to be able to show Luc my daily routines. But in each other's presence, the two Frenchmen could not resist ridiculing everything they saw around them. It began with the seemingly prosperous tree-lined college campus, which offended their French leftist instincts—such a contrast to the austere concrete buildings that typified the Sorbonne on streets of the Latin Quarter. One day I brought them both to the university's one cushy restaurant-style dining room, where students could eat lunch with their professors to discuss tutorials, theses, or simply socialize. This shocked them, as students in Paris affected much greater poverty, and their professors would never have mingled with them. Their mockery extended to the blueberry coffee cake I made them for breakfast (*not breakfast food*), the large cups of coffee (*big enough to soak your feet in*), and ridiculously large portions of mediocre American food served everywhere else. I should have guessed at how they would respond to my Maine fur hat: "At the Sorbonne you wouldn't have survived two minutes in that before someone stoned you to death!"

Although sometimes it was mildly entertaining, their constant belittling of everything American was inarguably offensive. I was angry at Luc for his insensitivity and refusal to insist on time alone with me. Although he was staying with me in my off-campus apartment where I lived with a roommate, after a whole day as a threesome with Philippe, I never had the feeling that we were alone. Romance and intimacy were hard to reestablish, although there were fleeting moments of closeness. One morning when I opened my eyes in bed next to him, he was looking at me intently and tracing his finger along my eyebrow. The visceral effect of that minuscule gesture nearly obliterated the rest. Being in love was a form of madness, that much was clear.

When my classes finally ended, we rented a car to drive to my parents' house in Maine for several days. I had wanted to show Luc the magic of a New England snowstorm, to climb the small mountain at Bates College near our house, and point out in the distance where I grew up as a little girl.

They got to witness a snowstorm all right—it took us more than six hours to drive up to Maine in a blinding nor'easter, and as I clutched the steering wheel of our rental car and headed into what must have seemed to Luc and Philippe like a Siberian wasteland, I sensed that the nightmare was about to get worse.

It was ludicrous from the start that I would be bringing my married French boyfriend and his lawyer friend to my parents' house in Maine. Luc had at first refused, saying that it wouldn't be right to put my parents in that position. But the Frenchmen had few options, since they didn't want to spring for a hotel in New York until the meetings the following week. Luc then suggested that perhaps my parents wouldn't have to know about our relationship, that I could introduce them as my two 'friends' from Paris. The notion that my parents did not already know every detail about my relationship with Luc, not to mention his wife and son, was absurd, as I had written ten-page letters defending and explaining the situation to them from the start.

Naturally, my parents weren't happy about it, but they were remarkably supportive. They could do little but trust me and hope for the best, knowing how in love I was. Even under these complex circumstances, my parents put their doubts aside and tried to welcome Luc and Philippe into their home. Their hospitality was met with cynicism and mockery. When my father took out a bottle of champagne to welcome the Frenchmen to Maine at our first dinner, Philippe murmured in an unkind aside to Luc, "This must be to toast *le mariage*." That my parents allowed us to share a room was yet another violation of propriety and only increased Luc's anxiety about expectations and answers. As Philippe arrived with a case of untreated conjunctivitis, my parents called in a favor from their eye doctor who made a special evening appointment to treat him, for which he showed no appreciation. One day, when Philippe awoke early and came downstairs alone, my mother pulled him aside in a whisper and asked him about Luc's marital status—an indiscretion which Philippe reported back to Luc, then Luc to me, and I back to my mother whom I ungraciously blamed for ruining the visit. The two Frenchmen never stopped bantering under their breath. Later I heard them mock my poor father when he took out a bottle of Mateus rosé wine with a twist-off cap, which, at the time, was the epitome of gauche.

After a few catastrophic days, the three of us flew from Portland, Maine, to New York City. Luc's schedule was dictated entirely by Philippe, who had planned the trip to fully exploit Luc's French tax-law expertise. It became clear that his so-called 'generosity' was nothing but manipulation. Luc's long days were consumed by endless meetings, and, although I was invited to join them for dinners, the work-related discussions continued. I never ceased to feel like an outsider. Luc considered Philippe a close friend and trusted him enormously. He never objected to the arrangement or to his lack of time to spend with me.

One night, Luc casually announced in a restaurant that he had lost the scarf I knit him, most likely in a taxi.

There was silence after this, then Philippe piped in: "You are crazy, you two." It became clear what he meant: that we were delusional to deepen this relationship when there was no future in it; that a twenty-one-year-old American flutist was fine for Luc to dally with in Paris, but in the real world, it was clearly better for the newest member of his father's prestigious law firm to remain married to the doctor from a respectable, French political family.

Another time, in the middle of the night, the phone rang in our hotel room, and I picked it up in a semi-conscious stupor. The two men reprimanded me like a child the next morning for doing so. The humiliation had reached a new level, and it was finally more than I was willing to tolerate. How I had lasted this long was hard to even fathom.

Luc had caught Philippe's conjunctivitis, so I waited with him for three wretched hours in a New York City emergency room. Finally, on the day of his departure, I sat on the bed of his hotel room and told him that our relationship was too painful, that he was giving me no indication that he would ever be free. I would start to see other people. It was over.

He broke down as I had never seen him do so, sobbing large wet tears into my shoulder, "Don't leave me . . . *please*. . . I am begging you. Give me more time."

I left Luc's hotel room, and, blinded by my own tears, felt my way down the hallway to the elevator. I crumbled against the wall as I waited for it to arrive. Luc followed and watched the doors of the elevator close after me. By now I had caught his eye infections. I was weeping audibly with red, inflamed eyes on a public bus in the middle of Manhattan. Men, women, and children were staring at me, and frail, old ladies holding large parcels were offering me their seats. When my parents met me at the train station in Portland, Maine, my eyes were frightening bloody slits, and I couldn't stop crying.

I was too upset to discuss what had happened, but my parents were hoping that the Luc chapter of my life was over. Another visit to the same eye doctor yielded ointments to cure what had turned out to be a triple infection.

Once I was back at school in January, surrounded by all my records and hundreds of Luc's letters, I wondered if I had been pretending the whole time—to my parents, to Luc, to everyone but myself. The visit had been a disaster and Luc's behavior inexcusable. But when I reread his old letters and listened to the music we shared, I had to resist getting sucked back in. How could I reconcile the immense discrepancy between Luc's persona in the aesthetic realm of his letters, poetry, and music, and the passive, insensitive one I saw during the trip? How had his common decency and understanding vanished? I was certain he would write to me, and when he did, I would not respond. I would use my silence as a weapon while I figured it out. That's all I had.

# TWENTY-FIVE

*Dear Julie,*

*I have begun this letter 100 times. Every day I write a new one, then tear it up; what is the fate of this one? Julie, I am completely destroyed since seeing you enter that elevator of the Dorset Hotel in New York. I have never known such a feeling of suffocation, of absurdity. In spite of all the little unhappy incidents of this trip that were tied essentially to Philippe, these days together in New York come back to me in their beauty, but in a foreshadowing of sadness that was to follow. I would have made the trip for one single look from you which remains precious in my memories. So next to that, nothing else mattered.*

*And since then, cold, unacceptable, inadmissible silence which cuts through me like an icy rain. I tried so many times to call you from New York, from Paris, no response; I have written, no response; I absolutely need to have news from you. Do you need guarantees of my attachment to you? My distress would convince you of it. Will you not respond? I am begging you. I wait for your news.*

*I shut my eyes and I wait.*

*Luc*

But I was unmoved, steadfast in my self-control. How could he glorify the trip when it had been a nightmare for me? What exactly about it was beautiful? Still, as I suspected, his words once again declared their power over me. But I sent nothing back in spite of the numerous letters from him that arrived weekly. This demanded supreme will power, as I had written every thought and emotion to him during the past six months. So I continued to write, as if in a journal, but mailed nothing. A dozen pages collected in my drawer. New letters from him arrived every day.

*Dear Julie,*

> *No news from you, so I write into this immensity that separates us. This silence is horrible, weighs down, and destroys me. To speak to you, just to speak to you.*
>
> *Come out of your silence, Julie, for me. I am asking you not out of selfishness but out of necessity, as I really feel that I cannot survive this silence. I have so much to say to you, I want so badly to hold you in my arms that I can only write with a broken heart and tears in my eyes. Please. I am begging you.*

> *Luc*

*Merde! Merde! Merde!* The memories of our romance were luring me back to him. They were too powerful for me to resist, and I was in his grip again. I still believed that I would never find anyone who would love and move me in quite the same way as when things were good, in Paris. It just wasn't possible that the Luc I had loved was gone. After weeks of receiving letters day after day, his words of longing, suffering, and attachment eroded my resolve. I sent the entire pile of my unsent letters that had collected in my drawer.

# TWENTY-SIX

---

*Dear Julie,*

*I must be dreaming. I just received your letters. How can I begin to tell you my emotion at so much suffering, sincerity, and love? Julie, you have given me a wave of calm and serenity. This deadly silence was killing me.*

*Know that there is someone in this world who is attached to you forever. Imagine these sobs on your shoulder in this sad hotel room in New York—I had been controlling myself for so long that I simply couldn't hold it in any longer. Julie, know that you have touched the deepest part of my cells, that you are inscribed in them biologically, in a way that time and distance cannot change. I love you.*

*Luc*

I had no doubt that I was perhaps under a sort of hypnotic trance. It didn't matter. I needed to see him again and give us one more chance. If it was going to end, I needed to do it my way, in Paris, without the meddlesome Philippe calling all the shots.

I withdrew my entire savings from the flute lessons I had taught during the year, and walked downtown to the travel agent in Middletown, Connecticut. Five hundred dollars bought me a round trip TWA plane ticket to Paris for my three-week spring break in March. The fact that I had earned this money gave me freedom and autonomy. Bad choice or not, it was mine to make. I didn't tell anyone. And I didn't tell Luc. Not yet.

I telephoned the *Chœur de l'Orchestre de Paris*. Miraculously, they were performing the Mozart Requiem during the dates I would be there, and I was given permission to sing in the concerts. Each night I fell asleep listening to this ravishing music, dreaming of being back in Paris, and singing in the chorus again with Luc. By the time it reached the *Lacrimosa,*[13] it had seeped into my dreams like a serum. I would erase the nightmare of December. Finally, after it had all been meticulously planned, I sat down with a piece of paper and my fountain pen.

"Dear Luc," I began, "I'm coming to Paris."

# TWENTY-SEVEN

*Dear Julie,*

*I just arrived at my office—another letter from you! My heart was pounding before I even opened it. But then to read this news! How can I describe what this has done for me—you cannot imagine! I have to reread your letter over and over to be convinced of it, it is so amazing. Paris in March, the beginning of spring. Singing Mozart together in the chorus. Julie, do you want to give me a heart attack? How could you consider wanting to surprise me?*

*Of course you can count on me at 7 o'clock at Roissy, Thursday, the sixth of March. I see Paris differently now knowing that in a month I will be with you walking around the streets we loved so much together.*

*Do you remember that Sunday morning in New York when we walked through Central Park, finally without Philippe, you with your characteristic walk and in that silly fur hat! And when you walked into deep, wet cement with your new boots on Broadway, instead of getting upset, you couldn't stop laughing? That morning I never found you more beautiful.*

*P.S. I found you a place to stay.*

*Luc*

CR

March sixth arrived. I packed only one worn leather satchel, the same one I had used for my flute and music when I first arrived in Paris. If I carried it on the plane, there would be no delay at baggage claim when I arrived. In it I had packed the minimum: a few changes of clothing, a book, my flute, and the music for my recital later in the spring. I wore jeans and a short leather jacket on the plane.

I drugged myself with Dramamine as soon as I boarded. The flight was half empty, and I was able to stretch out with a blanket on three seats as we flew across the Atlantic. I drifted into a light sleep for several hours. When I landed in Paris, it was 6:45 a.m., and Luc was waiting.

Once in his arms, I knew I had made the right decision. Luc held my face in his hands and looked at me with liquid eyes that spoke to me more than I could ever remember. He was attentive and quietly ecstatic. For the next three weeks I had no work, no classes, no obligations, and no plans other than to wait for him to come to me. So very early each morning on his way to work, Luc would quietly let himself into the apartment he had found for me near the Bois de Boulogne, and in the bluish silk of dawn, would undress and slip into my bed, his cool skin pressing against my sleepy warmth.

I never imagined I could be so blissful in this role of paramour, thinking only of when I would see my love again. I would linger in long, hot baths, walk around the unfamiliar apartment in a silk bathrobe that I found hanging on a hook, look in the fridge, listen to music, watch absurd French daytime television (usually decades-old American soap operas— Meg Ryan before she was famous), read, take walks, and practice for my senior recital. Luc would enter the apartment, fall into my arms and kiss me for a long time. He was more passionate than ever before, pressing me lustfully up against the walls and furniture, sliding his hands under my clothes once again after we had dressed, to find warm flesh and steal one more kiss before walking out the door.

Claire was now back in Paris doing her residency, and they were still sharing the same apartment, a situation which I believed was nearing its end. I was surprised to learn that Claire often referred to me by name, as Luc never hid the fact from her that he had an American friend in the chorus.

"Is Julie Scolnik coming to Paris in March to sing the Mozart Requiem or to see you?" she would ask. Or, "We should invite Julie Scolnik for dinner one of these days," she would taunt him. It was still unfathomable to me that the panty liner incident had not caused more of a rupture between them, and that they continued this charade.

I waited for Luc at restaurants at noon, met him when possible in the late afternoons, and several nights we went to chorus rehearsals to sing Mozart Requiem. We deliberately kept others guessing, as when a man in the bass section asked Luc, "Don't you know that girl in the soprano section over there?"

"Who's that? No, no I don't think so," was his answer.

But our time together was never without plenty of recreational bickering.

"I think you should thank Oldham for letting you sing in this concert," he said to me on our way to a rehearsal one night. "Yes, I would feel better if you did that."

I pounced, in English. "*You* would feel better? This has absolutely nothing to do with you. What does that mean, *you* would feel better?!"

There were endless other cultural clashes—he mocked and questioned dozens of things—why I ate my potato skin, or used a diaphragm instead of the pill.

"Why do you use this ridiculous piece of rubber, anyway?" He asked. "French women use the pill without a problem."

"That may be," I answered coolly as I brushed my teeth, "but everyone knows French medicine is backward." The word I used was *retardé*.

It worried me when these sides of him surfaced, but when he laughed and clearly enjoyed being challenged in this way, I knew things would be okay. We couldn't see eye to eye about everything—as long as we heard ear to ear. Like when I played him a cassette of a rehearsal for my upcoming senior recital, and he noted all my "magic moments" without my pointing them out.

On Saturday, the day before my flight home, Luc surprised me by showing up at my apartment with his toddler son, Yann. When I opened the door, there they were, standing side by side, holding hands. So it was true. Luc was a father. I had never seen him in this role before. Yann was wearing a tiny fisherman-knit sweater and had pale skin, tousled, light brown hair, and violet-blue eyes. I felt both unprepared and privileged to meet him. I knelt down to greet him. "*Bonjour*, Yann," I said, extending my hand. Luc watched closely, clearly moved to be bridging his two worlds.

"*Lui n'est pas gentille*—Him's not nice," Yann said, referring to me. Like most children, he seemed to have an intuitive grasp of dangers to his family.

"Speak good French, at least, Yann," said Luc. "Say *bonjour* to the Madame."

I hated being called *madame*, and was heartsick that Luc had a child with someone else. I wondered what a child of ours would look like.

"He's so adorable," I said, hoping to mask my envy and regret.

"People stop us on the street to look at him," Luc boasted, "and always comment on his eyes. Last night Yann took a huge book of law off the shelf and into bed with him, and was sitting up with it open on his lap, with one hand behind his head, as he often sees me do," Luc continued. "'What are you doing there, Yann,' I asked him. 'I'm reading,' he said, 'reading law.'" Luc beamed.

Anecdotes about his son sat heavily on my chest for hours. Each one painted a life in which I played no part. How could I compete with that perfect little boy? And how could I consider tearing this family apart? The more I heard, the more I saw the essence of the problem: Luc would never willingly miss a moment of Yann's childhood—and a divorce would make this inevitable. These three weeks together brought us infinitely closer, but as my spring break came to an end, Luc and I became miserably aware that we would be saying goodbye again, still with no answers about his working in the States, and ultimately about our future. We both felt the impending separation, the sense of dark, transient joy. But it was clear to me now: We would find a solution and be together. He would be free one day. I was willing to wait it out.

# TWENTY-EIGHT

*Dear Julie,*

*This morning I did not awaken you at dawn. Instead, I returned to my office where an enormous amount of work awaited me. "Don't be sad," you said to me in English, when you left at noon from the airport. These words are like blows in my head which all during the weekend came back to haunt me.*

*Dreams accentuate the frustration. This question that you asked: "Do you really think we'll be together again?" I cannot imagine for a single minute any other conclusion. I'll cross the Atlantic swimming, but I'll see you again. Send me news.*

*Luc*

*I lived remarkable days*
*That escaped like waves*
*Moving in great secret*
*And I found you lying down*
*In the shadows of this room*
*So you'd feel less alone.*

*The door opens and I slide into your bed,*
*A warm scent from your skin and your hair,*
*I feel your body, still.*
*And see the sadness of your face.*
*Your mouth seeks mine*
*And I find you beautiful.*
*Between my solitude and you*
*There are your eyes*
*Which close under my caresses*

☙

I returned to Wesleyan for my final months before graduation. Luc's letters had collected into a very fat pile, each folded identically in size and shape and stored in a Japanese rice paper billfold. Mixed in with the letters were three or four photos of him. One showed him lying down on my little bed under the eaves on rue Bonaparte, head propped up by one arm and making what looked decidedly like a French "u" with his mouth. Another showed him on a sailboat, balancing with his legs apart in tight black jeans and striped sailor shirt, while he helped maneuver some sails. These letters had become members of my family, my most reliable confidants, what I would run into a burning building to save. I would slip one out randomly from the middle of the pile, hoping it would contain something I had forgotten a little. I would read it again, then refold and put it back.

I couldn't stop thinking about the scarf Luc had lost in New York. Now that I was hopeful again about our future, there was only one way to get over my disappointment that the scarf was gone: I would knit him something bigger, something harder to lose: a sweater. I embarked on this formidable project as soon as I made the round trip to Boston again to buy the same blue-gray yarn. It was my first foray into something other than a scarf, and it didn't come easily to me, navigating the stitches and following a pattern. I found myself regularly in an emergency run to a friend's dorm after midnight to be rescued from a slipped stitch.

One Saturday night I had a surprise visit from Warren, the mysterious

Exeter crush whom I had manically avoided in Paris because of Luc. He was now back at Yale, just thirty minutes from Wesleyan. Warren had tracked me down, spontaneously showing up at my apartment on a Saturday night without calling, and I was home alone. I was thrilled to see him and it showed. There was still an undeniable chemistry between us, but I sent him quickly away, as I was locked in distant embrace with a married Frenchman three thousand miles away.

College was not supposed to be like this. My friends were making the most of the infinite intellectual, cultural, and social opportunities the school had to offer. By the time May arrived, and only weeks remained of my senior year, my classmates were all celebrating their imminent departures out into "the real world." But not me. I remained reclusive, pining and cloistered in my room. While they struggled with decisions about graduate schools and careers, only one question tugged at me day and night: How could I move to Paris to be with a married man?

I needed some reassurance. During one of my braver moments, I wrote to Luc and asked. I told him that I loved him and wanted to spend my life with him. Did he really see a future for us?

In my French Poetry class, we were studying Stéphane Mallarmé's *L'après-midi d'un faune*, the poem which inspired Debussy's famous *Prélude* that opens with a sensuous flute solo.

*"Aimais-je un rêve?* Did I love a dream?" I asked Luc, at the end of my letter, just like the faun who awakens in the woods and remembers the nymphs who surrounded him in his sleep.

# TWENTY-NINE

*Dear Julie,*

    *I met you when my life knew one clear and precise trajectory. I was enveloped in a structure whose only purpose was to contain my anxiety, sadness and my deep solitude. Life seized us in time. For me the essential question will always be, "Do you love me?" because only love will save me and not the institutional system.*

    *Therefore, I admit honestly that since your departure, I am truly distraught, but I scarcely asked myself the questions that you raise in your letter. It is perhaps tied to my temperament, but everyday life, that which is structured and conventional doesn't interest me. I escape to live in the imaginary, poetry, utopia, music, and dreams. You inhabit this world, Julie, and you are the only one, despite distance and time.*

    *This said, I don't know the future, and now less than ever, because I have never been so clueless about what awaits me on every level. I very much admire your "intelligence du cœur." Know that I am faithful (in the highest definitive sense) and that what Diderot called "cells of love" are of you; that is, they have invaded my being. Je t'embrasse,*

*Luc*

Not a single answer. A mastery of the French language so elevated that I hardly noticed. I was unequipped to see the control he had over me. Instead, I felt ashamed for asking for concrete answers, for not seeing that love was all that mattered. Of course, he was right, I told myself. I stayed by him.

Finally, a letter arrived with a surprise announcement: Luc was definitely joining the international law firm of Philippe's father, and as his need to learn English was even more urgent now, the firm was sending him to Berlitz in the United States for six weeks beginning in July. Boston was chosen over London because so much of Luc's work would be in America. They also knew that he had personal reasons for wanting to come to the States. Luc asked me if I could help him find a furnished apartment where we could live together.

Overjoyed at this news, I packed up my college apartment, opted out of my own college graduation, and devoted myself to welcoming Luc to Boston. With a serious mission now, and the prospect of a full six weeks together suspended brightly ahead, I made several long and grueling pilgrimages into Boston to look for a furnished apartment. Finally, a company called "Home Away from Home" showed me a clean furnished studio on Walnut Street, a beautiful small side street near the Boston Common. It would be only a short walk for him down Beacon Street and across the Public Garden to get to the Berlitz School near the corner of Boylston and Berkeley Streets. I couldn't disappoint him. The waiting was over.

# THIRTY

Dear Julie,

Thank you for all the work you did on my behalf to find us an apartment. The more I think about it, the more I think that the choice of Boston is an excellent idea. I am impatient for this trip, although I am extremely anxious about mastering the English language! Perhaps I will fail! But to spend the summer as a student under these conditions is really a dream . . . Imagine what that means for us. Julie, our encounters have sometimes been too brief to enable me to let go the way I wanted and needed to. We will finally have time.

I know you worry about Philippe, but please remember that my relationship to you has never been and will never be influenced by what Philippe thinks. Remember that it has been scarcely a year and a half since I met you and already there have been huge revolutions in my life that meeting you has brought about.

So try to stay calm and serene if you can. All that counts is what happens between us. Anyway, by July we'll be together in Boston and this time alone and tranquil. Remember that in July all will be possible. Stay calm.

CR

*Stay calm.* I repeated Luc's words like a mantra because the mere thought of his arrival made my stomach rile. We had never lived together. We had never had the luxury to be a couple. There were five free days after his arrival to spend together before Berlitz began, so I reserved a little bed-and-breakfast right near the beach in Ogunquit, Maine, a coastal town I knew well from my childhood. I imagined a mild ocean breeze blowing in through lace curtains, rousing us from our sleep. I couldn't wait to tell him about our plans.

Though he was flying into Boston later that day, I took an extra shuttle to New York in order to meet him sooner. I arrived two hours early, wearing a sundress, sandals, and a light vintage jacket slung over my arm. I had a tote bag full of things to show him: an article about Barenboim, a clipping from the New York Times about *Les Petits Chanteurs*, and a few other magazines I thought we could read together on the flight to Boston. The adrenalin spiraling through me was nearly incapacitating during my two-hour wait. When it got closer to his arrival time, I paced around the airport, checking the arrival announcements every two minutes. I couldn't eat and was weak with hunger.

Several times I went to the ladies' room, slurped water from the faucet with one hand and redid my hair clip. Each time I returned to the arrival screen, and when at last it flashed the latest information about the flight from Paris, I was horrified to realize that I was waiting on the wrong floor. I bolted down the escalator where clusters of people were already congregating by the ropes outside of Customs. Searching for an opening, for a spot where I could stand so that I wouldn't be lost in a mass of people, I frantically pushed and pressed through the crowds. It had to be a place where he would see my face right away when he came through the swinging doors. With relief, I found a spot. And then I waited.

For one solid hour I watched the doors swing open while people walked through to meet their loved ones—French grandmothers bearing gifts, hugging their daughters and grandchildren, businessmen kissing their wives and kids dispassionately after a routine trip overseas, and young lovers falling into each other's arms. My legs ached from standing so long with locked knees in my high-heeled sandals, and my shoulder blades burned from the weight of my bag. I felt icy cold and hot at the same time. My insides seemed to have disintegrated and I had to keep clutching my waist with my arms from time to time to steady myself.

It was June 26th. I hadn't seen Luc since the day I left Paris in March when my spring break was over. Every phrase he had written to me about the three weeks I had spent with him in March came back to me. Everything was clear, he had said, there was scarcely anything to say anymore. He had written: "*I see a time of certitude, you who know me as such a skeptic, for the first time in my life. Everything will be possible.*"

I tried to imagine his voice, to inure myself from the harsh, fluorescent airport. I breathed deeply, trying to slow my heartbeat. I recited inwardly my last few letters to him which I remembered word for word and pictured his reaction to each phrase. The last one had described the white silky Maine beaches where we would walk at night, listening to the violent roar of high tide. I couldn't wait to show him Maine's coastal ports, to show him how similar our childhood seaside settings had been, his in Brittany and mine in Maine, separated only by the expanse of the Atlantic Ocean. I imagined him on the beach wearing espadrilles like the ones I noticed in his photos from Brittany, and the blue-gray sweater I had finally finished and would give him that night. What would I look like to him as he walked through the doors?

Then suddenly there he was, coming through the double doors and walking so quickly in the wrong direction without looking up to find me that I had to struggle quickly through the dense crowds to catch up with him from behind.

But as soon as I saw his face, I knew that something was wrong. His brow was furrowed and there was panic in his eyes. I finally reached him, tapping him awkwardly on the shoulder from between clumps of travelers.

"*Ça va?*" he said without smiling or looking at me. I felt my body tense and the air choke out of me. Where was the movie embrace, the wild elation? His eyes were cold and distant, and he wouldn't look at me. I directed him toward the door, explaining in slow English what we were doing.

"You know it is midnight for me, so you might just as well speak Japanese—I wouldn't understand it any less," were his first words to me.

As we waited for a transferring bus, he asked, "You actually know what you are doing?"

I actually wondered *how* I knew what I was doing—traveling was stressful in general, and I was figuring it out as I went along. On top of that, Luc's behavior was making it hard to concentrate. His voice was remote. I scarcely recognized him. When the bus finally arrived, we piled into it with a dozen travelers. The driver rudely ordered people to move back and yelled out the stops along the way.

"Does he have the right to vote, that guy?" Luc asked. "One question I have," he said, "will I have a bed to sleep on tonight? Because I am absolutely exhausted." I told him that there was a convention in Boston and I had had a hard time finding any available rooms at all. The only one I had found with a vacancy had a single bed. He made an exasperated face.

I had hoped we could find an intimate place to have dinner and reconnect while we waited two hours for our shuttle back to Boston, but Luc said he didn't want anything to eat. When we arrived in Boston after our short flight, we took a taxi to the Park Plaza.

"Can you make sure there isn't another room with a bigger bed, or maybe even two beds?" he asked me.

"You know, I can stay in a different room altogether if you prefer," I answered, regretting that he could provoke me in such a way.

"I didn't travel three thousand miles to sleep down the hall from you," he said. Then, as we rode the elevator up to our room, I told him about my plans.

"You know, since the apartment on Beacon Hill isn't ready for us to move into until August 1, four days from now," I said, "I thought we could spend the next few days on the coast of—"

"Oh there's a little problem there," he said, interrupting me as we unlocked the door to our room.

"What do you mean?" I asked, holding my breath, feeling the blood rush to my face and my body stiffen.

He launched into a long explanation.

"I never explained to you that part of Philippe's plan was for me to stay in Boston for an extra week after my Berlitz course finishes in order to do some work for a Boston lawyer. This lawyer invited me to stay with him and his family on Cape Cod before Berlitz began. But I told him that I didn't have time."

I let him continue while disbelief built up inside me. Luc didn't know that besides booking a little inn, I had been researching the tide schedules, gallery openings, chamber music concerts at the local museum. I had been counting on this time to reconnect before he started his day-long classes at Berlitz.

"You know I cannot very well be rude to this man as his firm is in close contact with Philippe's firm," Luc continued. "And if I call him from Maine he'll know that I came early and didn't get in touch with him and that could create problems right away."

I took a deep breath, feeling shaky with hurt and rage.

"Luc. That was a nice gesture he made to you, but it was just a formality. I don't think he'll be upset if you don't take him up on his offer."

He continued. "Also, I cannot start spending money right away on a vacation. How much does the inn at the ocean cost? Then there's the bus fare, etc. After all, I came here to learn English. Yes, I could ask for more money for these weeks here but I don't *want* to do that. I have $1,800 but I have no idea how much that is, if it's enough or not. Tell me, how much money did you bring with you to spend? No, really, because we have to consider these things."

I was dumbstruck. I could have told Luc that I didn't expect him to pay for any of my personal expenses this summer, and that the money he was given by the firm would have covered plenty of extra activities to enrich his visit here. But I didn't. To have this discussion about money during our first hours together was extremely hurtful. I was silent for a minute. Then I tried once more.

"There will be plenty of time for you to get settled in Boston afterwards," I said quietly. "You knew you'd have to spend money on some kind of lodging when you chose the cheaper flight on Pakistan Airways, which arrived five days before the sublet was available."

"But there were other reasons to come early, *stupeed gairl*," he said. At last he acknowledged that he had come early to see me, but everything else he had said until now indicated that I played no part at all. I was feeling more and more shaken.

"But I made so many plans."

"Don't worry," he said, "don't get upset. We have so much time; we'll get to the beach."

Luc was distant and preoccupied, and even though he claimed to be starving, he rejected my suggestion to find a place to eat dinner and instead went straight to bed. I really needed food, but hardly knew what to suggest. I went to wash up, and when I came out of the bathroom, he was under the covers face down, with his head buried in the pillow. I opened my suitcase.

In a clear plastic bag on top was the finished sweater I had knit. Knowing I would regret it, I took it out. *Don't do it, don't do it!* I tried to stop myself.

"I knitted this for you," I said, in a flat voice, trying not to sound pathetic, "to make up for the scarf you lost."

He lifted his head and said nothing for a long time.

"It's such an enormous amount of work," he said finally. "You're crazy! But I have no room for it in my suitcase," he said. "Can you keep it in yours?" His face was back down in the pillow.

I thought back to all the hours I had spent knitting this sweater— during lectures, at orchestra rehearsals while I counted measures of rests, in my symphonic literature class, late at night in bed while listening to music. I folded the sweater and put it back in its plastic bag. There was no delicious anticipation that in a moment we would be lying skin to skin under the covers. I almost didn't dare take off my clothes. But I pulled my stretchy sundress over my head, slipped on a soft camisole, and was standing in my bikini panties. I slid into the bed carefully next to his body, trying to find space for my body without rolling into him. He turned toward me, and suddenly it seemed as if the bed had grown.

"The bed feels very big now," I whispered.

"Enormous," he said, almost against his will.

But it wasn't what I had waited for. He kissed me mechanically for a brief moment, but from worlds away. Then he turned his back to me and went to sleep. There was no passion, connection, or relief to finally be together after waiting so long. I barely closed my eyes all night.

# THIRTY-ONE

ON OUR FIRST MORNING TOGETHER, Luc and I didn't awaken languidly in each other's arms as I had imagined for weeks. He was tired, hungry, cranky; the hotel was second-rate, the bed too small.

I had just turned twenty-two. I had never lived in Boston and now that my original plan to go to Maine had been discarded, I really didn't know what to suggest. I felt too young to be in charge of all these plans. The language problem stripped Luc of all adult perspective and responsibility. We both needed real food but somehow ended up just grabbing coffee and a muffin from a bakery and an unripe peach from a fruit stand. I suggested we sit on a bench by the duck pond in the Public Gardens as I had done with such pleasure so many times when I came to visit friends in Boston. Luc hated the coffee and the unripe peach.

"This isn't a peach, it's an apple."

I couldn't think straight, as if I was suffering from some kind of concussion. Yet I rallied and came up with an inspired suggestion: to sit in on a class of English as a Second Language at The Boston School of Modern Languages across from the Public Garden. A good friend of mine from Wesleyan, Chiara, taught English classes there. I suspected this might make Luc feel as if he were getting a head start on what he had come to Boston to do. We walked down Newbury Street so that he could buy a card for his son. He said he hadn't properly explained why he went away. He scoffed at the designer clothing stores we passed. "What is this, the *Champs Elyssées?*"

The Boston School of Modern Languages was in an impressive brownstone on the corner of Arlington and Beacon Streets. I inquired in the office about Chiara Gabriele's English class. As we waited for the class to begin, we looked out through a window at the Public Gardens. It was a perfect summer day and all the tulips were in bloom. I looked at Luc.

"Luc, do you feel your arrival here has been anticlimactic?" I asked in English very slowly. He didn't understand the word 'anticlimactic' and thought I was talking about the weather. When I rephrased it in French, he answered, "I know *you* do."

I introduced him to Chiara, who spoke French to Luc to put him at ease, and warned him to be prepared to participate in class. "*Non, non, je vous en prie!*" He beseeched her not to call on him. The school bell rang, and we went to sit down in the classroom.

"We have two new students in our class this morning," Chiara announced with much animation. "Julie is from the exotic state of *Maine*, and Luc, tell us, where are *you* from?"

Luc turned red and responded in a barely audible French, "*Paris.*"

"PA-RIS!" she yelled out loudly in an exaggerated sing-song American accent. "Luc is from PA-RIS," she repeated, while every wide-eyed South American student turned around to get a better look at him. Luc barely opened his mouth during the rest of the class. We said goodbye to Chiara, with a plan to meet her in a few hours for lunch.

Luc needed to visit the real estate office to pay the balance on the rental and get his key. On the way, we stopped in the park while he wrote the letter to his son, which seemed to take an interminable amount of time. I tried unsuccessfully to focus on a newspaper.

"What did you write?" I asked as gently as I could, when he finally licked the envelope after about twenty minutes.

"Oh, you know, a child's letter. Very allegorical, with animals, and so forth, explaining why I went so far away. You know it's *much* more difficult to write this letter than the essay on Dialectic Thought I helped you with in Paris," he said harshly. Another kick in the stomach.

"Luc, can you try to talk to me, tell me what's going on? I know it was painful to leave Yann like this," I said. "But you were so excited about coming before. What happened? I want to try to help, but you seem to be playing some sort of—"

He interrupted. "I can't help it, *écoute*. This is my way of being, of existing. I can't do anything about it." He looked away. "Can we find a place to buy stamps?"

I told him we could buy some later at the small Charles Street Post Office. We left our bench and walked back to the language school to meet Chiara. As the three of us walked down Arlington Street, she and I began speaking English. We were translating everything into French as well, but Luc looked away and made it clear that there was no need to do so, as he had no desire to follow the conversation.

I was embarrassed by his behavior, but Chiara was a good friend. She suggested we have lunch at Souper Salad, a salad-bar restaurant that was quick, inexpensive, and nearby. I knew this would be extremely foreign to Luc, but decided to let him adapt. Chiara and I wanted salads, and besides, there were plenty of other things he could eat there like soup and quiche and homemade bread, and it was, after all, an American experience.

In the restaurant Luc looked lost. I tried to explain the choices on the menu, but he found me patronizing. "I can't just live on rabbit food," he complained. He refused to touch his soup, didn't know what to make of the salad bar, and was put off by my light-hearted conversation in English with Chiara. I could have brought him to one of the Euro-chic bistros on Newbury Street, where a steak and a glass of wine might have made him feel more at home. And I would have, but his behavior killed my desire to be kind and accommodating.

"When are you going to Maine?" Chiara asked us.

I didn't answer. Luc threw up his hands in a helpless 'don't look at me' gesture.

"Actually, I don't think we're going to go," I finally said. Chiara knew all about my plans to take him to Ogunquit, so this surprised her. When she realized we were temporarily homeless, she mentioned her parents were traveling, and offered to let us stay at their house in Arlington. I foolishly accepted.

That afternoon, after checking out of the Park Plaza, Luc handed me a twenty-dollar bill and asked if it was enough. I refused it. We took a taxi to a suburban neighborhood in Arlington, found the hidden key under a plant near the garage, and let ourselves into the house. I couldn't believe I had allowed this to happen. Being among total strangers' personal belongings made us feel like unwelcome intruders, and it only heightened the distance and awkwardness between us. A small bed-and-breakfast by the sea these four days would have made our reacquaintance so much easier. The attic room where Chiara instructed us to sleep was stiflingly hot with two tiny beds at opposite ends of the room. There was a huge heating pipe in the middle which obstructed the view from one bed to the other.

Luc collapsed on one of the beds and again announced how tired he was. I sat a moment on the edge of his bed while he searched through books on the night stand for something to read. The weight of my disappointment from his implacable wall of hostility must have poured from my eyes.

"They really frighten me, those eyes you have right now," he said.

I nodded. "They should," I answered.

He picked up a book and shut me out. My body felt leaden as I walked downstairs. I knew Luc would probably sleep for several hours, so I sat in the silent living room and tried to read. At around eight o'clock I went back up to the attic and sat on his bed and looked at him. The sweet summer air blew in softly through the open window, and I looked out at the milky blue light of dusk. I touched him gently, thinking it would be better for him to begin adapting to the new time. He awoke with a start.

"I didn't know where I was for a moment," he said. "I thought I was still in Paris. I am starving. Unlike you I can't eat a radish and call it lunch," he said, "or I'll soon die of malnutrition."

"There's lots of food in the refrigerator downstairs," I said, trying to start over and forget how crushed I was. "We can make a really nice dinner together if you want. You can even make yourself a steak."

"You should have awakened me after it was all ready."

In the kitchen we bickered about everything—about the pros and cons of eating red meat, about butter versus oil for stir-frying vegetables. He contended that since Americans were so fat and knew nothing about cuisine, they should not be giving advice about anything having to do with food and nutrition, and everybody knew the only way to make steak or vegetables was in butter. I disagreed, which drove him crazy. Thinking up clever retorts put him in the world he knew best. There were some laughs, but I wasn't having fun.

We sat down at the kitchen table without lighting candles or putting on music. Luc concentrated on eating and when he was done, he went up to the attic before me without cleaning up. It gave me a glimpse of what his marriage to Claire must have been like all those years. Maybe I had it all wrong. Maybe he was an unreliable narrator.

When I got upstairs, he was getting under the covers.

"Oh, *pardon*, I didn't ask you what bed you wanted," he said. I stared at him with disbelief. I got into the other bed and turned out my light. I hadn't slept well in two nights and fell asleep quickly in spite of my wretched state.

Our days continued in a mixture of excruciating boredom and contentiousness. I was shattered with disappointment, but I had been so convinced of my future with Luc that it was hard to process that I could have been so wrong. We took a long bus ride into Cambridge, and strolled around Harvard Square.

"*This* is Harvard?" he asked with the unpleasant face the French use to show they are unimpressed. Although I knew that none of our daily trials were my fault, Luc made me feel responsible for them all: that the bus ride into Cambridge was long and hot, that good art films weren't showing at the right times, that a dead fish was floating in the Boston Harbor, that inexpensive little bistros weren't materializing when we were hungry. We came across a little diner that I knew he'd hate but I brought him to it anyway. Afterwards, Luc said he felt poisoned by the food and was appalled by the overweight people he saw there.

"Look at them. They are so fat and they still keep eating like that!"

"You know, Luc, a lot of people with few resources are fat because they don't know much about nutrition and they eat at places like this because they're cheap," I offered, remembering his extreme leftist politics when he was in Paris.

"I don't have much money, either," he said, rising to my bait, "but when I was at the Sorbonne, poor students paid only two francs for an entire meal. I assure you that if the students had been fed this kind of food they would have staged a revolt! Forget May '68. This would have been more serious!"

On the way home we picked up some groceries. I rarely shopped for food or cooked for myself, with the exception of a very small repertoire, and was in no position to provide Luc the cushion of familiarity that he needed. I had never cooked a steak in my life, and hadn't an inkling about how to make any of the basic traditional French meals Luc was used to eating.

In the kitchen, I took out the Spanish onion and zucchini and began peeling the onion with a very sharp knife I found in the Gabriele's drawer. In two seconds I had brutally cut my left index finger. It was bleeding profusely. I didn't know how deep the cut was but the pain was intense. I grabbed several paper towels and wrapped my finger with them, then walked as calmly as I could into the living room, not wanting to deal with this alone. I sat on the piano bench and interrupted Luc's TV program.

"I just cut my finger," I said with a shaky voice and eyes about to overflow. He looked up at me, trying to decipher if it was serious or just a ploy to get attention. For a moment he said nothing. "If you want, I can take you to the hospital," he finally said with sarcasm, and then looked back at the TV screen.

"I don't know," I said. "I don't know how to tell how deep it is." I knew I sounded pathetic, but I needed help.

"Don't ask me," he said. "I'm not a doctor, and I don't know anything about that kind of thing. But if you think we should go to the hospital, we can."

I went upstairs to find a Band-Aid in the Gabrieles' bathroom. I was holding back tears from the agony of the cut, and on top of that, I always worried that a finger injury would interfere with the flute.

Knowing I'd regret it, I went back in. "Do you think you could help me with this?"

"*J'ai horreur du sang*—I hate blood, I don't deal well with it," was his answer.

I went back into the kitchen and wrestled with the bandage myself. My finger was trembling and throbbing, and the blood went right through the first two Band-Aids, so I added another. He was a monster. I despised him with every cell in my body.

During dinner when he noticed my bandaged finger he said, "It's interesting . . . but after living with you for a few days I notice that you completely lack concentration. It's very different from what I am used to."

For a moment indignation robbed me of words. I could barely breathe. "What amazes *me*," I said, haltingly, scarcely able to get my words out in French, "is that for someone who supposedly has a degree in psychology, you seem clueless about the connection between emotions and accidents."

"*Oh là là*, you certainly didn't appreciate that remark," he said. "*C'est pas un critique, écoute!* It's not a criticism! I wouldn't have said it if I had known you would take it this way. It's just an observation, that's all."

I stood to put my plate in the sink and knocked a pot off the counter. It landed on the floor with a crash. Luc stifled a laugh by covering his mouth and then threw up his hands as if to say, *I rest my case.*

The next day, Luc wanted to call Philippe to tell him that he had arrived, and asked if he could use the phone in the Gabrieles' house. The mention of Philippe's name made me recoil. I helped him with the operator and then went into the living room to sit on the couch. As I listened to his one-sided conversation with Philippe, I felt as if someone was squeezing the air out of my throat. I heard bits and pieces of his lies, one right after the other.

". . . yes I'm staying in a little inn. Yes, very much like where you stayed at that university . . . *oui, oui*, I saw Harvard today . . . very interesting . . . and everything is fine . . . *oui, oui*. Yes, I contacted a friend of hers who teaches English so I had a little head start on my English classes . . . Yes, things are very expensive here . . . yes . . . it's quite pleasant."

It baffled and stung me all over again that he felt he had to fabricate so many things. A big law firm like Philippe's father's would certainly have given Luc all the money he needed not to live in someone's tiny hot attic when studying English for his international work with them. Then I heard him get quiet and I guessed that the conversation turned to Claire. I heard Luc ask Philippe if it was not too much trouble, could he check up on her to see if everything was okay. Then Luc agreed that, yes, he should be the one to call her.

When he came back into the living room, I was sitting on the couch and fidgeting with a tortoise-shell barrette that I had just taken out of my hair. I was pinching the sides so it sprang open, then snapping it shut again. Open, close. Open, close. I couldn't speak, look up, or move. Open, close.

"Apparently Claire left Paris before her final exams," he began. "It worries me, you see; she was supposed to spend some time at Philippe and Francoise's house when the exams were over, and she didn't even warn them about her leaving."

I didn't know what he wanted me to say. That, yes, this was a bad sign, and he should call his wife right away in case Claire was contemplating suicide again? I never realized that he kept such close tabs on her. I kept staring down at my lap and playing with the closure of my barrette.

"Philippe told me to rent a boat and go up the coast," he said sheepishly. "But, Julie, just because he suggested it doesn't mean I would do it. It still goes against my nature to be spending money on a vacation right away. And he told me to go into as many stores and places as I could to practice speaking English with Americans."

There had been no mention of me to Philippe, nor the fact that I had planned just such a trip to the coast because I knew he would love it so much. There had been no mention that he was in good hands, since I had been trying endlessly to encourage him to speak English since his arrival. I kept staring down, and my hair had fallen around my face. Luc was watching me from a chair on the other side of the room. He was finally grasping that something was wrong. There was only the audible clicking of my barrette, open and closed. My eyes were filling up with tears and I knew that if I blinked just once they would fall in big droplets onto my lap. Open, close.

"What is it?" he finally asked. Slowly I stood and walked up to the attic, hoping that my loose hair obscured my eyes. I sat on my bed cross-legged and leaned against the wall. In less than a minute he came up and tried for the very first time to be attentive.

I tried to stop crying when I heard him coming and said nothing when he sat down on the bed. I caught a tear with my index finger and licked it off.

"Well *speak*, Julie, at least," he said, as if all this time I had been the one having trouble communicating. "Tell me what you're feeling."

I couldn't answer. My throat ached too much from trying to avoid sobbing. There was no way to make him understand. Where would I even begin?

"Don't you see how hurtful it is? Your lies, your need, like a child, to report back to Philippe . . . Why do you give him so much power? He knows you came here to be with me. Why is it so important to play this game and pretend I don't exist?"

"No, okay, yes. Philippe might know that I came to Boston to be with you, but I prefer not to bring you into the conversation any more, because since the trip to New York last December, when Philippe made his feelings clear where you are concerned, I no longer think of Philippe as a confidante."

I let it go. There was no use. We hadn't even begun, but there was no way to make him understand. When his meager momentary effort to reach me was over, he walked downstairs.

Chiara returned to her parents' home later that day with Hugo, her boyfriend, and I had to rally. Their car was filled to the roof with belongings that she needed to store at her parents' home for the summer. I went out to help her unload the car. When I saw Luc writing a letter in an armchair, I mentioned it might be nice if he offered to help, too. He put down his letter begrudgingly, annoyed to be interrupted, and went to the car to grab one small bag. Dropping it on the floor with the others, he then went back to his chair.

I glared at him. This couldn't be the same man who took time off work to help me move in Paris. Back then, he drove his little Volkswagen up onto the sidewalk next to the open French windows of Madame Cammas' apartment, and lifted my suitcase, boxes of music, books, and knick-knacks through the window and into his car. He had insisted that I take every last stray Chianti bottle-vase of dried flowers, and lined them all up on the floor of his car, telling me not to worry as we bumped along in his tiny car, reassuring me that they would survive the journey across three *arrondissements*. And when he pulled into the courtyard of my new home at 8, rue Bonaparte, we took the bottles out and placed them upright on the small round roof of his Volkswagen, while he carried all of my other belongings upstairs to my tiny maid's room on the sixth floor. We had stopped at the landing on the fifth floor, and looked through the window at his car in the courtyard, its rooftop a garden of dried colored fingers reaching into the gray Parisian sky, and we had smiled at this random, displaced charm. After he carried everything up for me, including every bag of useless chestnuts that I had collected from one of the parks, he asked me if there was anything else I needed, then kissed me goodbye, and said, "I'll come by to get you tonight for the rehearsal?" And when he left, I collapsed on my new, unfamiliar bed, but felt certain that I was loved.

But that Luc had disappeared.

Chiara pulled me aside and tried to console me, telling me not to make any demands on him and to relax. She suggested I help her make dinner with Hugo who had just bought an excessive pile of ripe bananas at Haymarket for a dollar. There was also a plate of freshly roasted and salted cashews, a bowl of raspberries, a pot of coffee, and a disorganized array of coffee cups.

"We roasted cashews in butter!" Chiara announced happily. "Have some raspberries," she said to us.

"Is this their dinner?" Luc said under his breath in French to me when he came into the kitchen. I shrugged my shoulders, trying to ignore him. Then he added, "What, they eat all the time, you mean?"

Chiara's free and relaxed manner made me realize how tense I had been and how I desperately needed to be with friends. Seeing me connect with them only alienated Luc further. Chiara announced that she wanted to bake something with all the bananas, but needed to find the perfect recipe, and began pulling down cookbook after cookbook from the shelf, sliding her finger down each index, looking for recipes. Layers of books were left open all over the table, and they buried the plates of cashews and raspberries

In the middle of cooking dinner, I decided to call home. I went to the small den where I could shut the door. I knew my parents were in for a surprise.

"Hi, Julie! Are you calling from Ogunquit?"

"Hi," I answered flatly. "No, we didn't go."

After a moment's pause, my mother began again, carefully.

"You . . . what? You didn't go at all? Where are you? Are you in Boston?"

"No, we're at Chiara's parents' house in Arlington. We decided to wait for a while before going to Maine, until we've seen some of Boston first, since we won't have time once Berlitz starts," I lied.

"Gee, that's too bad," my father piped in from another extension. "All week we've been saying to each other, 'The weather is so ideal for Julie and Luc at the ocean. They're so lucky to have so many perfect days in a row.'"

"Julie." My mother's voice was lower and softer than usual, and I could tell she was trying hard to control all the questions she wanted to ask. "Tell me this: why did you change your mind?"

"I dunno," I answered, annoyed by my mother's perceptiveness. "I guess we'll go another time. There's a lot to do here first, and since Chiara's parents are away, we're using their house. We might go to Tanglewood."

"Do they know you're there?"

"It's hard for me to answer all your questions," I lashed out. They tried to take a step back.

"We were hoping you'd call, Julie," my father stepped in. "We were wondering how things were going. How's Luc?"

"Fine." There was silence on the other end. They knew.

When I hung up I felt worse. Speaking to them made the devastating last few days become real, less like a bad dream from which I might still awaken. But it helped to know my family was there if I needed them.

Chiara was in the kitchen preparing a chicken recipe with Hugo, taking down multiple spices from the cupboard, rendering the counter a chaotic sea of ingredients. As the evening progressed, Luc withdrew more and more. I tried desperately to have one moment of eye contact with him, to let him know that I understood how he felt, that I was disappointed, too, to have lost our privacy. But during the entire evening he avoided my eyes, even when we passed each other in the hallway.

After dinner, without a word to anyone, Luc went upstairs to the attic. I told Chiara and Hugo I would clean up, and when they were about to leave, they asked if I was going to be alright. I exhaled a shaky breath, and said I was okay. When the door closed behind them, I felt my body go limp. I slumped to the floor against the front door and closed my eyes tightly, trying to hold back the tears. They welled up quickly anyway, and I covered my face with my hands, wondering how I would survive another night.

I went into the kitchen to do the dishes, but my finger was still throbbing, and I didn't want to get my Band-Aids soggy again. I tried to maneuver the sponge with only one hand, but gave up after a few dishes. Besides, the darkness outside the kitchen windows frightened me and reminded me of why I hated babysitting in strange homes as an adolescent.

When I returned to the living room, I walked past a wastepaper basket and noticed a pile of small torn pieces of paper at the bottom. It struck me as odd, so I reached in and pulled out a handful of them. They were covered in handwriting which I knew intimately. My heartbeat increased when I realized these were the remnants of a letter Luc had begun to Claire. I dumped the tiny pieces on the coffee table, turning some over so that all of the writing faced up. *I'm doing a jigsaw puzzle*, I thought.

I couldn't piece it together completely, but I was able to make out a few words on one piece: *seul et perdu.* *"Alone and lost,"* he had written to a woman with whom he had claimed to be estranged for a very long time. A few larger pieces seemed to go together: *". . . must be hard to be a doctor."* I had never heard Luc express respect for Claire or her work in any way. And the last sequence: *"when I get home . . ."* as if he were away from her now against his wishes, and counting the days till his return to France. As if he needed someone to confide in. But even more than reading these hurtful phrases, the world of letters was a universe that belonged to *us*. I felt as though I might be sick. My eyes closed again. I hugged my arms and bent over to console myself. But the letter was torn up. Why?

I turned off the lights downstairs and climbed the stairs to the second-floor bathroom. I washed up, replaced my Band-Aids again on my still-throbbing finger, and looked in the mirror. I barely recognized the thinner, tear-stained face looking back. There was no glimmer of a smile or light in my eyes. I tried to remember that people found me pretty, because all I saw now was a miserable, dejected girl who didn't know what to do next. Climbing the attic stairs, I prepared myself for more of Luc's icy presence in the far bed.

I undressed in the dark, quietly throwing my clothes on top of my suitcase. My long hair fell onto my bare back and shoulders when I took out my hair clip. This fleeting moment of sensuousness made me achingly aware that I hadn't been touched since Luc's arrival. From my suitcase I pulled a frayed button-down sleep shirt that I had pilfered from my dad's giveaways. When I climbed between the cool sheets, I turned on my side, tucking my wrists, catlike, under my chin as I curled into a ball. The tears came back quickly now and I couldn't stop them. I reached for my purse in the dark and took out my pocket Kleenex, blew my nose quietly, and took the packet of tissues to bed with me.

When I awoke in the morning, Luc was standing over my bed. He looked at the sea of used tissue balls on the floor.

"What did you do last night?" he asked.

My lashes still wet from a fresh morning cry, I didn't look up at him. Finally, I sat up against the wall and faced him. After the fiasco of the first day when I tried to immerse him in English, I only spoke French to him now.

"Luc, why are you here?" I asked very calmly. "Why did you bother coming here? I don't know how to live with you like this . . . I don't know *how*, do you understand? I know how foreign everything is, and how alienated and panicky you feel, but what I can't understand is this side of you that I have never seen before, the scorn, the coldness, the complete lack of . . . " I looked up slowly as I tried to find the word I wanted without sounding trite. ". . . love."

*"Mais non,"* he said, unconvincingly.

"Look," I said, "I'm not saying this just so that you'll give me words of reassurance."

"I know that," he said coldly.

"But I should tell you," I continued, "I am ready to leave." More tears welled up.

"Don't *cry*, Julie," he said, more with impatience than compassion. "I really regret that you're respond—"

"You *regret?*" I squinted at him. "You sound as if you had nothing to do with these tears!"

He sighed, and paused. "What do you want me to say?" he asked. I didn't answer.

"Yes, it's true that since my arrival," he continued, "I haven't yet adjusted to the time difference, and I am somewhat depressed, but *you* shouldn't fall apart simply because I am having a difficult time."

"I shouldn't . . . *fall apart?*" I said. My throat constricted again from trying to hold back the tears and I couldn't continue. I waited until my vocal chords relaxed enough to be able to speak again.

"You don't understand," I said in a shaky voice. "Besides, I'm thinking of the bigger picture now. We're too different, our needs are too different. Even if you weren't acting like this now, we could never be happy—not now, not in two months, not two years from now."

*"Bon, d'accord,* okay, yes, that I understand, I see what you are saying now." Another blow.

"All those feelings we shared, Luc, those elevated feelings, during the concerts and during English lessons in Paris; you can have them all back. I am giving them *back* to you. They mean nothing to me now. I would choose never to have experienced any of that in order to not live through this now."

Luc glanced down at the monogram on the pocket of my father's frayed shirt.

"*Christian Dior,*" he smirked, as he turned and walked downstairs.

I forced myself to get out of bed. It was the first time in my life that I had to will myself to function: to breathe in and out, to put on my clothes. I went downstairs to wash up. I had only one thought now—to leave the Gabrieles' house in impeccable condition and put the key back where it was supposed to go, and get us out of there. When I came downstairs, Luc was in the living room again, reading.

"What happened to Tanglewood?" he asked.

"We missed the bus," I answered flatly.

"Good work," was his answer.

That night in Arlington, there was a program on public television about the pianist Arthur Rubinstein. A summer electrical storm had just erupted outside, and the rain was coming down violently. Rubinstein began playing the slow movement of Chopin's second piano concerto,[14] a piece we used to listen to together, kissing languorously by candlelight in his apartment. It seemed like a lifetime ago. I wondered for a second if the music might help bring Luc back to the place he felt most at home. I wondered if it would bring him back to me.

"This has to be one of the saddest melodies ever written," I said, when the introduction was over and the main affecting tune began. I got up to sit on the floor in front of the fire I had lit.

Luc continued to stare at the TV screen. "Very romantic music. *Too* romantic," he said, as if trying to resist how it made him feel. I stared at the flames, letting my face get hot and tingly red. When I turned away, the cool air of the darkened room soothed it. All at once I was overcome by an escalating rage I couldn't contain. I stood and walked toward him, determined to do anything I could to make him react. I tried to grab his arms. He responded with twice as much strength, blocking me with his hands and holding mine back. I couldn't move.

"I hate you, I *hate* you . . ." I said, sobbing. For the first time in my life, I understood crimes of passion. With a weapon in my hand, I don't know what I would have done.

# THIRTY-TWO

"WHEN ARE YOU GOING TO London?" I asked my mother in a tiny voice from the phone in the den of the Gabrieles' house.

"Not till next week," my mother said calmly, waiting.

I paused. "Do you think it's too late for me to come with you and Donna?"

"Not too late," she said. No questions asked. God, I had great parents.

"I'll call you in a day to confirm," I said.

"We'll come pick you up," my mother answered. And we hung up.

The next day, after straightening up the Gabrieles' house, and putting the key back in its hiding place, Luc and I took a taxi into Boston with our suitcases. The moment we arrived at 7 Walnut Street, Luc wrote "Berthelot" on a small piece of paper and slid it through the rusted metal rectangle underneath the mailbox marked 4D.

"I may be getting mail here, too," I said matter-of-factly. He begrudgingly added "Scolnik" in much smaller letters beneath his name.

Although the rental was just as I had remembered it, seeing it now in my current state was such a stark contrast to the excitement I had felt when I first imagined living there as a happy couple.

The next day, Luc awoke early to get ready for his first day of class at Berlitz. He emerged from the bathroom dressed in a crisp, white shirt with a navy-blue sweater slung over his back, his wet hair neatly parted and combed back. He looked like a nervous French schoolboy as he paced back and forth in the apartment. I almost felt sorry for him.

When he left, I was relieved to be in Boston now and on my own. I wasn't sure what the next day would bring, but for the moment, I wanted to enjoy Boston and focus on my own life and interests. I decided to invite an old college flutist friend over to play duets. Then I took my flute to the flute shop to be cleaned and adjusted. On the way home, I looked at everything with forlorn irony—the swan boats and family of ducks in the pond of the Public Garden, the small sailboats on the Charles River. It wasn't supposed to be like this. I wasn't supposed to be this sad. At six o'clock I sat on our designated bench in the park and waited for Luc, bracing myself for more disappointment.

Luc arrived looking drained, but surprised me by making an effort to speak English for the first time. I tried to start over, to forget all the heartache from the previous days. I was patient and gave him time to find his words. He kept sighing deeply, as if begging for sympathy for his hard day at school. I was neither prying nor attentive, and instead talked cheerfully about my day.

"I had my flute fixed today," I said. "It needed some adjustment and plays so much better now. I found out about an organization called the National Flute Association, which is holding its annual convention in Washington, D. C., this summer. And I'll probably go—August 17 to 19."

This made him turn his head. "What do you mean?" he asked.

"Which word don't you understand?" I answered, enjoying the effect this was having on him.

"*C'est quoi, ça?* What *eez zat*, a flute convention?" he asked.

"Oh you know, a kind of *congrès*, probably lots of concerts, newly published flute music, I suppose, well-known flutists, exhibits, a chance to visit Washington. Do you want to come?" I asked innocently, knowing how he would react.

"*Non*, of course *not*," he said in English, with a strong French accent. "First, I am not *flutiste*, second, I do not 'ave zeh *monay* to go to Washington. I come to Boston to learn English."

"Oh that's too bad. I'm definitely going," I said as I ran across Charles Street.

"What days are *zey*, 17 to 19?" he asked, still thinking about it ten minutes later.

"Oh a weekend, of course," I said casually.

"But *sree* days?"

"Friday probably," I said distractedly, letting him know what a small role he played in my plans. Psychology 101.

When we got back to the apartment, he immediately sat down to watch the news. I managed to come up with a simple dinner and we ate like strangers confined in distant worlds. How Claire could have lasted as long as she did with him was unfathomable.

He sat down in front of the TV. When a commercial came on, I had nothing to lose.

"Luc, I need to talk to you."

"Not now."

At that moment he gave me no choice: I would leave the next morning. I took out three sheets of paper and my fountain pen, and for the next hour wrote him a goodbye letter in French, as I lay on the bed just a few feet away from where he was sitting on the couch.

"What are you doing?" he asked dryly at one point, looking up for a second from the screen.

"Writing you a letter," I answered. "You can read it if you want." *One. Last. Chance.*

"Not now," he said.

When I was done, I folded the letter in half and put it in my suitcase.

The next morning I awoke feeling numb but resigned. I was already gone. There were no more tears. I wasn't conflicted anymore. I lay on my side under the covers, one arm tucked under my head, and looked at him. He opened his eyes, and managed a small uneasy smile when he saw me.

He checked his watch on the night table, sighed heavily, then got up and went into the bathroom.

"I forgot to buy coffee," I said to him as I slid my jeans on, "so I'm running down to Charles Street to get us some." This wasn't a gesture of kindness; I just really wanted coffee.

"Well, if you're going to do it," he said, through the closed bathroom door, "you better be fast, because I don't have much time."

I threw on my clothes and ran out, hastily buying two large coffees, a half melon, and a blueberry muffin for him. It was odd to be buying him a muffin, just minutes before leaving him forever. As I was coming back up the stairs, Luc was closing the door of the apartment behind him and would have left without a word, had I returned one minute later. I handed him one of the cups and he reluctantly came back inside. We sat down at the small dining table. He grimaced at the first sip. I held mine with two hands, both elbows on the table, while I took grateful gulps and looked out the window. Seconds later he stood up, grabbed his notebooks and went toward the door. My back was to him. *He has no idea.*

"See you tonight," he said impassively. I didn't answer.

He took a step back into the apartment, as if puzzled by my silence. He came around to see my face, which was fixed on a tree outside the window. I took my eyes off it momentarily and looked at him blankly while one hand lifted from my cup in a mock, ironic wave. And then he left.

I sat for a moment, sipping my coffee and staring out the window. *After all the memories,* I thought, *this is the last image I will have of him.*

I hadn't unpacked so there was little to do. The sweater I knit remained in its plastic bag, neatly folded at the bottom of my suitcase. I showered, packed up my toiletries, flute, and music stand, and then reread my letter numerous times until I knew it by heart. I made the bed neatly, then carefully placed the letter, folded once, on the pillow. I looked around. There was no trace of me anymore in the room, except for the four white roses I had bought and placed in a tall thin glass on the night table. The petals were beginning to droop slightly, their faces lonely and sad, like lost souls in the world, just as all my roses eventually did in my Paris *atelier.*

Exiting the elevator with my suitcase on the ground floor, I remembered to cross my tiny name off the rectangle of paper beneath mailbox 4D. I knew this is what he'd see first when he came home and checked his mail. And then, so that he would never wonder if I were coming back, I threw my set of keys into the mailbox, slammed the narrow door, and drove away with my amazing parents who had come to rescue me.

I sat silently in a state of shock as I looked out the window from the back seat of the car as we drove up to Maine. My parents didn't ask me any questions or try to find out what had happened. For two hours I recited the letter silently to myself, word for word, while I imagined Luc sitting on the bed, holding it in his hands.

*Dear Luc,*

*Letters have always played a fundamental role in our history. This one is no exception. But after the hundreds that I have written to you, this is the first that is not a love letter. And it will be my last.*

*I am leaving you, Luc. You deserve no explanation, but I will finally make you listen.*

*The person I loved is gone. You disappeared between the last letter you sent and your first steps off the plane. I will never understand how you could treat me the way you did. But I cannot spend another minute bewildered about how I could have been so wrong.*

*I won't talk about Beethoven's Ninth or Brahms Requiem— music which tied us, as Proust wrote, like the "national hymn of our love." I won't remind you of your grandiose graduate thesis about the humiliation of women—your empty, hypocritical belief that no human being should tolerate humiliation of any kind. All I can say is that I have never in my life felt more humiliated by someone than I have during these past five days. By you.*

*I am certain that you will attribute my leaving to some deep flaw of mine—that I lack discipline or give up when things get tough. Believe this all you want. Unlike you, I see no reason for two people to share a kitchen, a living room, not to mention a bed, if there exists nothing between them. Detachment comes more naturally to you than connection; you have perfected it your whole life. As for me, I will not beg for love, nor will I ever accept to live without it.*

*I had thought that this love story was timeless and wouldn't end in disillusionment like in books, films, and songs. For a year and a half I dreamed and waited and I truly believed I wouldn't have to give up my idealism. But I was wrong.*

*And if that were all. What a fool I was to believe that one day you would be free. It is clear now that you were never going to change your life for me.*

*I can no longer say that I regret nothing. I regret every kiss I placed on your lips and every tear I shed missing you. You have left me a wound that will remain in me for the rest of my life.*

*I will never understand how so much love can disappear in five days.*

*Julie*

Living well might ultimately be the best revenge, but imagining Luc sitting on the bed reading my letter would suffice at that moment. He had told me that Claire often threatened to be gone when he got home, but she always returned in tears, unable to leave. He must have believed my threats were just as false.

I tried to make sense of it all, to figure out what had happened. In Paris, just months earlier, he was full of the compassion, consideration, and sensitivity that had always characterized him. Even letters that I had received just twenty-four hours before his arrival were full of affection and unbridled enthusiasm that we would finally be together.

Suddenly, with his first steps onto American soil, some kind of chemical metamorphosis occured. Stripped of his native French language, his 'raison d'être,' he was immobilized with fear and assumed a callous contempt for everything around him, including me.

But there had to be more to it than that. Was he suddenly overwhelmed with new waves of guilt both toward his son whom he left for the summer, and toward me, too, for whom he still had no answers? Had something else happened recently that I didn't know about? Was there pressure from the new law firm to stay married to the doctor from the famous political family? Did he deliberately act like a beast so that I had no choice but to leave? I worked hard to come up with these rationales. How else could I explain where the love went?

My mother and sister let me tag along to London where they had planned a week-long trip to see English theater. I knew how privileged I was to take such a trip, especially at the last minute, though it wasn't extravagantly planned. We stayed in a small hotel (I slept on a roll-away cot), and saw wonderful plays by The Royal Shakespeare Company, as well as new productions by Tom Stoppard and other new playwrights. I consumed pots of English tea, trays of Cadbury biscuits, and distracted myself further by wildly perming my hair.

I couldn't get over how the world around me looked the same when everything inside me had changed. In the middle of the night as I lay on my back, tears ran silently down my temples as my mother and sister slept nearby. It was a different sort of pain from when I was pining for him. No, I hated him with every ounce of my being. I was still in shock from his behavior, and for the moment that's all I felt, as if trying to emerge intact from a gruesome accident.

But as I flew back to Boston where I was to begin a new life, I couldn't stop thinking about how hopeful I had been. The summer had transformed me. There was a gnawing whisper in me that I would never feel the same way again. Wordsworth said it best in "Tintern Abbey": *I cannot paint what then I was. That time is past and all its aching joys now no more, and all its dizzy raptures.*

Was nothing that he wrote me true? Or was love something so fragile that it could turn to dust just like that, in the course of a few days? Phrases from all his letters I knew by heart played incessantly in my ears, like a tune I couldn't get out of my head.

*. . . Paris loses all meaning for me now that you are gone, and I have the impression that I am floating in a kind of unconscious state. Julie, I know that you felt my difficulty to communicate. This is an old problem of mine. With you it seems I have more ease and our connection transcends my coldness and inhibition. Your open personality and your obvious intuition about me can help me find paths to a more intense and ardent communication with the world.*

But he was wrong. I thought I could coax him into the light, but even I failed.

# THIRTY-THREE

I PUT DOWN THE FIRST and last month's rent on a charming, high-ceilinged studio with fireplace, hardwood floors, and bay window in an old Boston brownstone at 274 Clarendon Street. The rental fee was $275 a month, which I knew I could manage with private students and the teaching job I got right away in the Preparatory Department of the New England Conservatory. For weeks I had no furniture except a mattress on the floor. In time, I found a chest of drawers, night table, and dining table in used furniture stores and yard sales, and I bought a brown chenille sleeper sofa which I pulled out into a bed each night facing the fireplace, often lit.

One night in September, I was coming home with a bag of groceries when my knees went wobbly, and I felt as if the muscles in my arms were leaking out through my elbows. Since my move back to Boston, I had deliberately avoided calculating whether Luc was still in town finishing up his Berlitz course. I was still somewhat shell-shocked, and had squirreled away the facts in a tiny little box which I buried, and tried not to think about. But from out of nowhere, the exact date of his return flight to France resurfaced in my memory. It was September 12, and I was nearly certain he would be leaving Boston the next day. I climbed the wide staircase to my studio, unlocked the door, and put down the groceries. When I stood in front of the mirror over the mantel, my eyes looked glassy and wild. My long hair was wild, too, still recovering from my post-break-up perm. Scarcely aware of what I was doing, I turned out the lights, slung my cross-body bag diagonally over my shoulder, and ran down the stairs. Hurrying, afraid I might lose my nerve, I jumped on my bike, and rode to 7 Walnut Street, the Beacon Hill address where I had lived with Luc for those few days.

A few minutes later I was pressing the small white buzzer of 4D. A clean new rectangle of paper under the mailbox now read only "Berthelot." I didn't know what I was going to say, but I knew that whatever happened in the next few minutes, he would be returning to France the following day. And I would never see him again.

My heart bumped around my rib cage when I was buzzed in right away without having to speak through the intercom. The adrenalin surge nearly incapacitated me as I rode the elevator up to the fourth floor and knocked on 4D. When it opened, a smallish brunette was standing in the doorway. My first thought was that Luc had left Boston early and that new tenants had moved in.

"Oh, excuse me, has the other tenant left this apartment already?" I asked her.

The woman looked confused and apologetic, and responded in a thick French accent. "*Pardon, excusez-moi* . . . can you speak . . . *moaure* slow pleeese . . . I . . . do not *ondairstend*."

"Does Luc Berthelot live here?" I tried again. Who *was* this woman? Was it his sister, a friend? Had he met someone new? As unlikely as that seemed, even more improbable was the thought that struck me next like a bolt of lightning. In an instant, it was at once shocking and crystal clear. My mind flashed back to the portrait of the woman hanging in Luc's Paris apartment.

This was Luc's wife standing before me.

# THIRTY-FOUR

LUC WAS NOWHERE TO BE seen. *Too late to turn back now*, I thought, as if I had just stepped off the diving board and in mid-air knew that only the icy shock of the water awaited me.

"*Bonjour*, I am Julie Scolnik," I said politely in French, extending my hand and expecting to see some recognition. She was tiny—I noted her narrow hips and petite-size jeans. At five-foot eight and in high-heeled sandals, I towered above her as I entered the apartment. Her face was pretty, tired, and sad. She wore no makeup and her hair was in a messy ponytail.

Claire shook my hand, but her face registered nothing. I was taken aback by her feigned ignorance. Did she play the same games as Luc? She knew who I was—the American girl in the chorus whom she often referred to by name as a way to provoke him. Even though so much must have become obvious to her at that very moment, she pretended to know nothing.

"Do you know my husband?" Claire asked in French now, finally emerging from her stupor. "Have you known him for a long time?" She continued more aggressively now, her questions coming in quick succession without waiting for answers. "Were you friends? More than friends?"

"I'm so sorry," I said, choosing my words with surprising composure since I was quaking inside. "I shouldn't have come here tonight. I had no idea. But the past is irrelevant now—the important thing is that there is nothing between us anymore," I said. "I almost wrote to you," I continued, knowing I was going too far.

"I wish you had," Claire said. "I suffered a great deal this past year."

"It's not my nature to hurt people," I said, now that I saw Claire standing before me. "If I had known more of the facts . . . I mean, I believed your marriage was over long before I met Luc."

The front door opened and in walked Luc, carrying a pile of folded laundry. The loathing in his eyes slapped me across the face as soon as he noticed me standing there. *Definitely French movie material*, I thought, even in my shaken state. He shut the door behind him.

*"Julie Scolneek."* He said coolly in his strong French accent. He didn't flinch. This was self-control on a pathological level. I wanted to slap him.

"Yes," Claire piped in. "We've been chatting for several minutes and things have become very clear. Very quickly."

Luc said nothing and his face was a mask of composure. Evidently he hadn't explained anything to her. She must have suspected a great deal about why Luc came to Boston in the first place, but must have been puzzled as to why he invited her to join him. But there was no proof. Until now. This was the last piece of the puzzle, delivered to her on a silver platter when she least expected it.

"Sit down," they both said to me, in canon, standing on ceremony at a time like this, as if I had stopped by for tea. *Oddly enough,* I thought, *'standing on ceremony' now involved sitting.* I was motionless, except for my left fingers which fidgeted with the strap of my shoulder bag. Interminable seconds passed. I couldn't think of what to do or say, or how to run for the door. Luc was standing facing me, and Claire had backed into the couch where she curled herself into a ball like a cornered animal. I knew she was a brilliant doctor, but all I saw was a scared and injured woman trying to process the scene before her. She could see my face but not his. I looked directly at Luc.

"I shouldn't have come tonight. I'm sorry. I had no way of knowing that . . . I only remembered that you were leaving tomorrow and came to wish you *bon voyage.*"

"*Merci beaucoup,*" he said with venom. His mouth was tight, clenched.

For a split second I turned toward Claire and considered saying, "*Enchantée,*" but thought better of it. I stole one last look at Luc's stone-cold eyes, and with an "*au revoir,*" was gone.

I ran down the three flights of stairs and out into the cool fall air, my rapid shallow breaths emitting a tiny whimper as I struggled to unlock my bike and straddle the seat. I teetered unsteadily down the uneven bricks of the Walnut Street sidewalk, then turned right and sailed down the steep incline of Beacon Street, my helmet dangling clumsily from the handlebars. But there were no tears. I felt empowered. Thankful to be riding away, leaving it all behind.

At last I saw that Luc and Claire were a couple. I never really believed Claire was real until that moment. As long as Luc was writing me love letters, she didn't exist. In one fleeting second, I exposed him—and oh-so-innocently—the night before his return to France. What a scene I must have left behind as I closed the door to their apartment, Claire yelling, crying, accusing; Luc, shutting her out and refusing to discuss it. It was their problem now. At least I would never again be on the receiving end of his loathsome behavior.

I started to imagine how it was possible that Claire had come to join him. In spite of his despicable conduct towards me during those five days, he must have felt even more panicky to be alone after I left. He must have called Claire when the shock had worn off, and said, "Why hadn't I thought of it before? Why not come spend some time in Boston with me and have a little vacation for yourself while I finish my Berlitz course?" And Claire, hoping that perhaps this was a new beginning for them, accepted.

೧೮

I wondered whether I could make use of my French while I networked and tried to break into the Boston music scene, so I decided to look for a teaching job at a language school. I went out and bought a trendy little suit at Lord and Taylor—a charcoal-gray pencil skirt with a fitted matching jacket, and set up an interview at—where else—the Berlitz School. I was aware of walking through the same doors that Luc walked through every day that summer.

The interview, in French, went fine, but they informed me with ample condescension that they only hired natives as foreign language teachers. They could probably use me for ESL, English as a Second Language, they said, if I went through the training. As I was leaving, I lingered by the main desk at the front entrance.

The man behind it looked up.

"May I help you?"

I hesitated. "Um, yes . . . I was just wondering . . . Did you know a French student from the summer named Luc Berthelot?"

He looked at me more intensely. "Oh sure, he was one of the smartest students we ever had here," he answered.

It infuriated me. How could they know how smart he was? He had no knack for languages.

"Did he actually learn to speak English?" I asked, unable to let it go. I wanted the man to say, *"No, unfortunately, he never really grasped it; he had a terrible mental block and couldn't get past his dreadful French accent. In fact, something happened in his personal life after only a few days which seemed to render him too emotionally distraught to finish the course."*

"Oh yes, absolutely," the man replied. Then, with curiosity, "How did you know him?"

I thought about what to say. That we used to be madly in love and sent hundreds of trans-Atlantic letters to each other when we were separated for a year? That I was certain he was the love of my life, but when he finally arrived in Boston to study at Berlitz, it was over in five days?

"I knew him in Paris," I said.

# THIRTY-FIVE

I NEEDED TO SETTLE INTO my new city, take auditions and launch my career. But I wasn't ready. I sat in silence for hours at a time, doing nothing, waiting for nothing. When would I stop dramatizing this? I was not the first person to suffer from heartache. How long would it take for my life to turn this wretched corner?

When I took the Red Line from Charles Street Station to Harvard Square, and the subway rose above ground as it crossed the Charles River, my body ached for the vastly more beautiful old bridges of the Seine, and for the life that I had imagined there. *I'm never going back*, I heard myself say. A door had shut. Open it now and I would find no enchanted garden.

Needing to make sense of what happened, I bought three spiral notebooks, filled my fine-tipped fountain pen with brown ink, and walked to a bench on the Esplanade by the Charles River. In a random mix of French and English, I wrote quickly with cramped, ink-stained fingers, and when one notebook was filled, I began another. It was as if I needed to empty the archives of my heart where all the memories, the good and the bad, needed to be unearthed. As soon as I met Luc, in January of 1977, I had stopped writing in my journal, convinced that any effort to articulate any of my transformative emotions was unattainable. But now here I was remembering entire conversations word for word that had taken place eighteen months earlier. How was it possible that it all came so effortlessly? I was simply transcribing onto paper hundreds of details and verbatim dialogue that were already etched indelibly in my memory.

Capturing with words the endless facets of our early romance kept it alive a little longer before I hammered the last nail on its coffin. I wanted to remember it all and yet, as I wrote, all Luc had given me and all he had taken away came together at once in a weight that was impossible to bear. Each day I walked to a different bench by the Charles, or in the Boston Public Garden, and wrote for hours, my eyes flooding and smudging my ink.

I tried to practice, but I couldn't play my flute without my throat seizing and tears leaking from my eyes. Almost all music tortured me, but I found it physically impossible to listen to any of the pieces deeply rooted in our history, pieces that we had loved together—the Brahms and Mozart Requiems, the Andante movement from the Schubert Bb Piano Trio, Jean Ferrat's *Les Poètes* from his love poems of Louis Aragon. I was sick with memory if I tried.

> *Did you listen to the Jean Ferrat record? Did I advise well on which one to buy? Ask me to explain the parts you don't understand. I listened to them last night, the songs set to Aragon love poems, and imagined you listening to the same ones 3,000 miles away. I am going to see Ferrat soon. What can I say to him after all these years? That there is an American girl on the other side of the world whom I love and who listens to his songs alone in her college room?*

Months later, a letter in a light blue airmail envelope arrived in my Clarendon Street mailbox. The return address said *Claire Berthelot.* I stared at it for a long time trying to process it.

It was startling to be holding a letter from the woman whom I had considered for so long to be the sole obstacle to my happiness. An elegantly hand-written letter in French, asking me for help. I had to look up dozens of words, but even then, her complex sentence structure required multiple readings to understand its nuances.

"I am writing to you because I need help assessing my own past and future with Luc," she wrote. "I need help deciding whether to leave him." She was asking me to write a letter outlining the nature of my relationship with Luc during the past year and a half. Claire also wanted to know how his behavior had prompted me to leave him after only five days. Her letter was very civil, stating that she had no unfriendly feelings toward me, quite the contrary.

Still driven by vengeful rage towards Luc, I wrote that letter. I strove to match Claire's eloquence as I described what I considered pertinent information—how we had met, my limited understanding of their marriage, why I left him. Miraculously, it was returned to me because of an error in the address, and by then, I had come to my senses. And it wasn't because Luc had found my phone number and called me at 3:00 a.m. a few weeks earlier asking me not to communicate with Claire.

"I don't owe you anything," I had whispered to him, sitting up in my sofa bed in the dark.

I sent back a brief note to Claire stating that I had received legal counsel (my father, a judge), and could not risk becoming involved in their complicated divorce proceedings. I was sorry.

Another letter arrived two weeks later. Would this never end?

*Bonjour Julie,*

*I am terribly sorry that you refuse to help me. A single word on your part would suffice to spare me great torments, such as the custody of my son, and many other things as well. I understand intellectually your refusal and I know that Luc found your phone number and threatened you. But I don't understand your refusal on a moral level. You did, inadvertently, contribute to the failure of my marriage with Luc. Now I have decided to leave him—something that has become extremely difficult because of his opposition to it. I think that there is no equal measure between the problems that you can help me avoid and the possible ones that Luc could cause you.*

*I see only threats that might justify your refusal to help me; empty threats, in fact, since in a court of French law, no witness in a divorce case is obligated to appear in person. It is enough to redirect one's testimony with a photocopy of an ID. Therefore, no witness falls under French jurisdiction. I beg you to keep this letter a secret and I hope that you understand that I am sending it to you as one sends "a bottle to the sea."*

*Claire Berthelot*

It was an excellent letter, I had to admit. But I was in over my head and couldn't take any chances. I imagined receiving a subpoena to testify in French court. Let them fight it out, I thought. It wasn't my problem anymore. I wasn't remotely affected by Claire's attempts to make me feel guilty. But there was one phrase that slugged me anew in the pit of my stomach: "*. . . because of his opposition to it.*" He was opposing the divorce. Even after everything, it made my head spin.

I spent another few weeks finishing a rough version of this saga up to the present time, autumn of 1978. I even gave it a title: *Lilies that Fester*, from Shakespeare Sonnet No. 94, which I included on the inside cover.

But it was time to put the manuscript away. Scribbling for weeks into the notebooks was cathartic, but now it was time to stop. I put the three journals, the two-inch thick pile of his letters, and the photos of him all into a shoe box, and slid it onto the top shelf of my closet. I hoped this act of writing would help me move on.

It did not. I bought a paperback at the Harvard Bookstore called, *How to Fall out of Love*. It suggested snapping a rubber band on one's wrist each time that person came into one's mind. This also did not work.

Luc didn't disappear from my thoughts all at once, but a little at a time, like a photograph that fades a bit each day when left out in the sun, or a seaport that grows smaller and smaller as you drift in a boat out to sea. But after he left my conscious thoughts, he would return in my dreams. And, strangely enough, it was often in the form of the scary flying monkey from *The Wizard of Oz* that I had associated with Luc even back in Paris, when he smiled broadly while delivering an ironic retort. It was only by remembering former dreams and putting all the pieces together that I was able to figure out that they were all about him.

In one nightmare, I was in a crowded room filled with clusters of people, a cocktail party of sorts. Suddenly this flying monkey creature entered, but in this version, he stood upright, and was taller and broader than a man. A hush came over the room of people as he appeared in the doorway. There seemed to be an expectation that it was up to me to do something—I had a knife. But I couldn't move, so I passed the knife to the girl on my right. She raised the knife and threw it forcefully at him. But he was clever and caught it instead. And now he was angry, furious, and prepared for revenge. His face contorted in vicious laughter, and mocking us, he threw the knife back at her. It landed in the recess of her white throat where a brilliant red blood erupted. I awoke, shaken and disturbed by the violence.

But in another dream months later, there were many smaller variations of this same creature, and they maliciously blocked and confronted me, laughing at my despair. I was late to a concert, needed to get somewhere, but always, these creatures stopped me. I fought them off the best I could, until it seemed that only one remained. He ceased his jeering and was no longer fighting me. Curled instead into a kind of fetal position on his side, he was clutching his knees with his arms. I approached what now had become a scared, vulnerable, and passive creature. And then, as I enveloped and comforted him in my arms, he transformed into a nine-year-old boy, in flannel shorts, knee socks, and pullover sweater. He was a *Petit Chanteur,* a little boy soprano. Luc at age nine. That was the hardest part to leave behind.

# Part Three

# THIRTY-SIX

❦ ❧ ● ❧ ❦

THE NEXT TIME I SAW Luc was five years later, when I took a trip to Paris with my boyfriend, Jimmy, a soft-spoken, balding flute player with whom I had been living dispassionately for several years. Our days were spent practicing flute repertoire in separate rooms, or, if together, the difficult Flute 1 and Flute II runs from Ravel's *Daphnis and Chloé Suite,* volumes of Kuhlau Flute duos, or the double-tongued flute duet from *A Midsummer Night's Dream.* It wasn't long before we were two very busy, boring, freelance musicians living glumly in a basement apartment on Gloucester Street in the Back Bay. We didn't own a car, and although we could have rented one or taken a train to picturesque New England destinations, we never ventured out of Boston or interrupted our gig routines. Seasons were distinguished not by ravishing foliage or snow-covered mountaintops, but by whether we were playing Tchaikovsky's Nutcracker Ballet or Bach's Easter Oratorio.

I had had passionate love and saw how that played out. Being with Jimmy was proof of how I had matured. This was the life I had to accept now; there was nothing else. At least I knew that my flute playing would benefit. The sweater I had knit for Luc became the "Luc sweater," that Jimmy, friends, and family would all borrow for years to come.

But I was often miserable, and being with someone whose entire life revolved around a tube of metal was suffocating me. Not surprisingly, Luc never completely left my thoughts. Jimmy had never been to France, and although I suggested a trip there as a chance to broaden his horizons and introduce him to Paris, I secretly wanted to stage an encounter with Luc to show him that I had moved on. And I would do it with a meticulously schemed appearance at a chorus rehearsal.

I made all the necessary inquiries regarding the Orchestra of Paris chorus schedule and got permission to sing in a rehearsal. They were working on Mahler's Second Symphony, the "*Resurrection Symphony.*" I bought the score and recording and learned my part before we left on the trip.

One night I unkindly left Jimmy at our small Left Bank Hotel and retraced the familiar metro route from Saint Germaine-des-Prés to Porte Maillot. When I arrived, I chatted nervously with old acquaintances, too terrified to look over at the bass section. After ten minutes I finally dared to look up across the chorus at the men, but I didn't see Luc. I scanned the rows over and over but no, he wasn't there. It was impossible! I had planned this encounter without knowing for sure if he was still a member of the chorus. But I turned my attention to the entrance of the rehearsal hall, and just seconds before the pianist played the first chord, he came waltzing in briskly and sat down.

I could barely hold my music. Filling my lungs with enough air to produce a sound was out of the question. But when I made a feeble attempt to join the other sopranos, I looked up over my score, and there he was, above the conductor's waving arms, that same blurry figure in the background that was carved in my memory. And minutes later, as if time didn't exist, our eyes locked.

When the rehearsal was over, he approached me cautiously, his shoulders as tight as his mouth, his hands stuffed into his pockets.

"*Ça va?*" he asked, without warmth.

I shook my head. "*Toi?*"

He nodded back. "Can we get something to drink?"

"I'm sorry, no, I can't. I'm with someone," I said. *Three thousand miles to say those words.*

He was quiet for a second. "Can I give you a lift then?" he asked.

"No, someone's waiting for me," I lied.

"*Tant pis, alors*," (Too bad, then) he said, shrugging his shoulders and turning away.

I left alone, hurrying out before him. I ran quickly up the stairs and out the stage door. And then, instead of heading toward the metro as I usually did, I ran onto the crowded intersection of Place de la Porte Maillot. Standing at the center of the busy rotary, facing Avenue de la Grande Armée, I felt panicky and overwhelmed by the many massive boulevards branching out in every direction, like spokes of a wheel. There were no taxis anywhere in sight and small French cars sped by me in the dark, as my throat constricted and tears welled up quickly in my eyes.

I had hoped that seeing me would hurt Luc. But after that evening, I found no satisfaction or relief from that small act of revenge. I was unbearably distracted during the rest of my time in Paris with Jimmy. As I walked around all my old neighborhoods during the next few days, my hidden histories with Luc arose from every corner. Like frozen footprints in the snow. How could I stop remembering how happy I had been with him on these same streets?

Moments before leaving Paris, while Jimmy was still up in the room packing, I came downstairs to check out. Our taxi was already idling on the sidewalk in front of the hotel. With an involuntary glance up the stairs to see if Jimmy were coming down, I entered a tiny phone *cabine* in the lobby without thinking and dialed Luc's number at work. I asked for him exactly as I had done hundreds of times in the past when my eleven o'clock call was the highlight of my morning.

"*Allô, oui?*" He answered with very little inflection. Nothing came out when I opened my mouth.

"*Allô?*" He repeated. More seconds passed.

". . . It's Julie."

There was a long silence and then I continued.

"I am leaving Paris in a few minutes," I said. There was more silence.

"Can I write to you?" he asked. "What is your address?"

I told him. And we hung up.

It was significant that I didn't feel the slightest bit guilty for betraying Jimmy in this way. What I *did* feel was idiotic for making such a massive transcontinental effort to prove that I had moved on. But I also knew that calling him two minutes before leaving Paris told him a different truth. Five days later, a letter arrived:

*Dear Julie,*

*It is difficult to retie a thread interrupted for five years as if time didn't exist, as if everything sent us back to a connection instantly reestablished. Furtive encounter. Sudden, unreal. I try to understand its meaning as one would analyze the symbols of a dream. The second symphony of Mahler, the "Resurrection" Symphony. Is it an accident? I don't think so.*

*The eyes, especially the eyes. For the rest, no time to see, to contemplate it, to speak. The music will provide that. Across the piano, one look among a hundred looks. Strategy will be stronger than all logic, but only for a time, for then there was the telephone call from the hotel (at the very last minute).*

*Logic prevails over strategy. So it is possible to talk. It is possible to see each other. We will talk. We will see each other.*

*Je t'embrasse,*

*Luc*

I knew it all so intimately—the handwriting, the paper, the lyrical phrases. It was like being reunited with a long lost relative. And like hundreds of his other letters, this one got under my skin. I was stunned by the power of his written words to draw me in again so forcefully. The music of his voice played in my head and acted like a password which accessed all my former feelings despite our shocking ending. Luc was like a sorcerer who could pull me under his spell with his prose. He could reach me in a way that no one else could. *Maybe if I never read his letters,* I thought, *maybe I can escape.* I tried to convince myself that even though I was unhappy in my current relationship, Luc was just a reflection of my own desires, a figment of my imagination. His innate poetic qualities appealed to my romantic vulnerability. *It isn't real,* I repeated over and over. The Luc chapter of my life had ended miserably that ill-fated week in Boston. There was no going back. It was over. *Over.* I forced myself to remember the man I had discovered. I didn't write back. But my heart was laid bare.

Jimmy and I parted ways soon after. Five years of living spiritually and emotionally stifled in a basement apartment playing flute duets was penance in the prime of my twenties, and I was ready to emerge into the sunlight after years of living in a cave. I had just discovered the novels of Colette, and identified with her free-spirited, zealous women. They exuded a conviction that life was short and was meant to be embraced with passion. It was time to enjoy a world that I had been kept from appreciating for so long.

Primed for adventure, and now sexually literate, I traveled to Europe, had a few daring escapades (beginning on the airplane), and even returned to Paris to play a concert. I was propelled by a determination not to feel locked out of this luminous city in spite of my painful history with it.

For the remainder of my twenties, I had many more disastrous relationships with a variety of men—a macho, mustachioed flute-maker who made me a beautiful rose gold head-joint but left me feeling vacant, a yuppie architect across the hall who complained that I was privy to all the "pieces" of his life, a lawyer turned macrobiotic yoga-fanatic who gave his dog acupuncture, and was forbidden by his Chinese doctor to lose his *vital essence,* and a computer graphics mountain-climbing Vermonter, the injured son of two alcoholic parents, who dumped me on a bike ride by the Charles River. Joni Mitchell lyrics played constantly in my head: *". . . There's a jouster and a jester, and a man who owns a store / There's a drummer, and a dreamer, and you know . . . there may be more."*

I had tried hard with all of them, to no avail. Though none were married or French, not one of them made me see my future children in his eyes. That is, until Michael came along.

# THIRTY-SEVEN

———— ⊸≋≋⊷ ————

SIX MONTHS AFTER MY THIRTIETH birthday, on a bitterly cold
December night close to New Year's Eve, I had joylessly ventured out of
my cozy studio on Beacon Hill to meet my friend Arlene for Thai food
in Cambridge. As usual, I was wearing my Russian fur hat with its points
side to side, like Napoleon, instead of front to back. As I climbed the
subway stairs, and headed toward the smaller of the two Harvard Square
newsstands, Nini's Corner, suddenly there he was—a gorgeous, intellectual,
twenty-something with a large head of unruly waves—heading there,
too. He was holding a nylon duffle bag with dress shoes protruding out
of half-closed zippers, as if he had come straight from the airport, and
was a terrible packer. We found ourselves standing side by side looking at
magazines, and I was keenly aware of him.

A voice behind us announced to a friend, "Look, the new *Scientific
American* is in," and we exchanged amused glances. His green, sparkly eyes
immediately made me squirm, and I left without buying what I had come
for, regretting that in my greatest moment of need, I hadn't been able to
muster my most natural gift—initiating a conversation. I fled the scene
and ended up at an underground discount record store nearby, where, after
perusing the bins distractedly for just minutes, I decided to go back to the

larger newsstand across the street, *Out of Town News,* to finally make my purchase. The cutie-pie duffle-bag-guy appeared out of nowhere just as I was about to go inside and pay.

"Do they have better magazines at this newsstand?" he asked me with just the right touch of irony, and a smile that I suspected I could look at for fifty years. I chattered away, a great contrast to his relaxed, gentle, and self-deprecating manner. I would later learn that he saw my Russian fur hat sailing across the intersection and decided to follow me to the second newsstand.

He was heading to Grendel's Den with his *Time* magazine, he said casually, and asked if I cared to join him. I walked him to the bar but I had to leave right away for my dinner date. Without exchanging numbers, he suggested we meet the very next night at the same time and place. It was a brilliant plan. No awkward phone calls to make or receive from a virtual stranger whose name I didn't even know. Of course, it could have ended like the movie, *An Affair to Remember,* with one of us getting hit by a taxi, and the other never knowing what happened.

But it didn't.

We met the next night and the night after that. And very soon it was clear to me that Michael was the person I could love with all my heart for life. We courted and married in an October evening candlelit ceremony eighteen months later. In the midst of our vows, we held hands and listened to friends play the bittersweet *Adagio* from Beethoven's E flat String Trio.

"*Grow old along with me. The best is yet to be,*" I said to Michael, placing a ring on his finger, as he nodded with dancing eyes, encouraging me to continue.

"*This is my beloved, and this is my friend,*" he responded, sliding the ring onto my finger. We stomped on a glass, danced into the night to a live Klezmer band, and squeezed our eyes shut when friends swooped us up in the air on chairs.

We flew to Italy for our honeymoon, and ate *zuppa di pesce* in the narrow streets of Portofino. Our hotel in Venice looked onto the windows of La Fenice Opera House, and from our bedroom we could hear the singers rehearsing Rossini's *Cinderella.*

"You're going to be such a good mother," my new husband said to me when I offered him almonds and raisins from my bag just when he started to feel a bit peckish on a bobbing gondola.

Michael didn't write poetry or love letters the way Luc had, but every cell of his body incarnated his attachment to me, and every day his small and large actions expressed his love in the present, physical world. He didn't share Luc's passion for music, but my sweetheart could lull me to sleep with a few magical strokes of his fingertips on my forehead, and our limbs interlaced like baby animals when we slept. He rated the severity of my chronic back injuries by number (*That looks like a seven to me*), directed me back home every time I got hopelessly lost in my car on a flute job (pre-GPS), and patiently initiated me into the daunting world of computers by making a numbered list that began: "*1. Turn computer on,*" as he would do in later years with cell phones, palm pilots, iPods, digital cameras, and countless other gadgets that were techno-challenging to me. When we were trying to have a baby, he lifted me by the ankles after love-making to increase the odds of conception. Months later, when I was pregnant and sleepless, he ate bowls of Life cereal in bed with me at 2 a.m., and after our daughter was born, stuffed pillows under my elbows to ease back pain when I was nursing.

Michael never tried to discourage my chocolate addiction, knew not to kiss me on the lips right before a flute recital, and could make me erupt into laughter with a single facial expression that poked fun at one of my inherent, quirky personality traits. He had a deep sense of humanity, a luscious libido, and a naturally athletic body. He accepted and embraced my unfettered, free spirit which was so far from his own rational, scientific mind. We shared countless, intimate details and humor about the everyday pleasures and complexities of our lives.

Shortly after we married, we moved to a narrow townhouse on Dana Street in Cambridge, just a ten-minute walk from Harvard Square. Michael was head of research at the Union of Concerned Scientists, and I had become a busy and successful Boston musician, juggling numerous principal flute orchestra jobs, teaching, giving recitals, and running a house and family.

And then, one Friday morning in December, the phone rang. I picked it up as I slid a tray of blueberry muffins into the oven.

"Hello?" I said breezily.

"*Bonjour. C'est Luc Berthelot.*"

# THIRTY-EIGHT

---

THE VOICE WAS DEEP AND velvety, like an old record I knew by heart, but had kept in a trunk in the attic.

"Hi!" I opened my mouth to say more, but nothing came out.

"*Bonjour* . . . I am here in Boston on business and was browsing through the phone book," he said in French, "and came across your name. '*Tiens,*' I thought to myself. 'There is Julie Scolnik's number.'"

It was an odd way to admit that he had looked me up. You don't just stumble across a name in the phonebook.

It had been almost fifteen years since that fateful summer when I threw my keys into the mailbox of the Beacon Hill apartment, ten since I had dragged Jimmy to Paris to show Luc I had moved on. I was happy now, secure, and fulfilled in my marriage, with nothing to prove anymore, and no false acts of indifference to orchestrate. It would be fun to see him, and I didn't feel ashamed or defensive about wanting to.

I drove to the Marriott Hotel at Copley Place, left my blue Volkswagen Beetle out front with the valet (*had I forgotten that he had a blue Volkswagen, too, in 1977?*) and darted into the lobby to find him.

"*Comment vas-tu?*" he asked with a big smile as he kissed me on each cheek. "You seem well!" he said, delighted to see me looking so healthy, happy, and confident. This was the charming Luc I remembered from the beginning.

"I'm a much better version of my former self," I laughed, trying to imply a great deal more. *Better because I'm not with you. Better because I am not under your control. Better because I am in love with a multifaceted, brilliant, kind man who can give me so much more.*

"I can see that!" he said, laughing.

He had a free day until his flight back to Paris in the evening. I had no way of reaching a private student that I was scheduled to teach at my home, so I suggested that he come back to Cambridge with me, and that we meet for lunch after the lesson. We walked out to the front of the hotel, where I unlocked the passenger side of my small, disheveled car, and tossed a music stand and a Boston Ballet Flute I part in the back seat to make room for him.

As we drove over the frost-heaved Cambridge roads, Luc couldn't stop smiling, seemingly amused to see me driving. He touched the back of my neck from time to time.

My student wasn't due for another half hour, so I invited him into our house on Dana Street for a cup of tea. I felt exposed but pleased as I led him into the sweet little home that I shared with my husband and two-year-old daughter, Sophie. We walked through our compact living room past the pine hutch, chenille couch, and shelves of books and records next to the fireplace. On the mantel was a menorah with candles burnt low, and two framed photos—one taken moments after our wedding ceremony, as Michael and I took long hopeful strides away from the crowd, and the other of Sophie in a Halloween cat costume. A short, bushy Christmas tree with filigree Balinese ornaments stood in the bay window, and an upright parlor piano in the opposite corner. I led him into our kitchen so I could put on the kettle. I watched Luc take it all in, the crayon drawings pinned on the refrigerator with heart-shaped magnets, the gingerbread house crowning the dining room table.

As I was pouring the tea, Sophie returned from a walk with the babysitter, Dee.

"Have you two been playing outside?" I asked them as I picked Sophie up, spun her around, and kissed her cold red cheeks. I was the one with the small child now, and I couldn't help thinking back to the time I met Luc's small son, Yann, in Paris. Sophie and Dee went upstairs to read and do art projects. This would have been my practice and teaching time. The phone rang and Luc heard me accept a concert engagement and saw me write several dates into my agenda.

I felt glad that he was peeking into my life, as if it might be a first step towards putting things right somehow. But without ever having had a real conversation about our ending or the intervening years, I knew it would be impossible to get there.

As we stood in the kitchen drinking tea, I wanted to say it all now. There was no danger of misunderstanding, no risk of saying too much.

"There were so many times when I thought about you over the past fifteen years," I said. "Did you ever see the film, *Cinema Paradiso?* Do you remember the middle-aged man who returns to the Italian village where he lived as the little boy, Salvatore, the one who loved movies?"

Luc nodded.

"The older Salvatore," I added, "the one who comes back, he reminded me of you when I saw it."

"I heard the Ninth Symphony the other day," he added timidly, as if it were now his turn, "and it reminded me of when we sang it."

"Luc." I stopped for emphasis. "I think about you *every* time I hear Beethoven's Ninth," I stated as a simple fact, not to provoke or flirt, but to mock him for pretending that it wasn't a given. "The Boston Symphony closes its season with it every summer at Tanglewood," I continued, "and I sub with them quite often."

"Some clients brought me to Tanglewood a few times," Luc answered. "I looked in the flute section but didn't see you."

Why was this so hard? How exactly were we meant to bridge this massive chasm?

When my student arrived, we made a plan to meet for lunch at a Japanese restaurant in Harvard Square, and Luc left to walk there on his own.

As we ate sushi and slippery udon noodles, we tried to chat casually, but our conversation was forced and unnatural. I learned he never remarried after divorcing Claire, but had a daughter from another relationship which had since ended. He had become an exceedingly successful lawyer, the head of one of the biggest firms in France. *Le patron,* the boss, he said. He helped support his parents and his siblings, and besides the apartment he owned in Paris, he had a house in Provence.

Knowing I would regret it, I tried to bring up that fateful week in Boston, saying that it was my innate mental health that made me leave after only five days. His face barely acknowledged what I was talking about. I saw that trying to get him to discuss it with me now would be like asking him why he couldn't see reds or greens. He simply couldn't. He raised his eyebrows at some people laughing raucously at a nearby table.

"Nothing has changed," I said, shaking my head. I was so frustrated by my inability to crack his wall, that when he asked me what I was currently doing with music, I was the one who wouldn't answer, except to say, "It really doesn't matter." Then almost under my breath I said, "Only connect."

"*What?*" he asked.

"It's a quote by E.M. Forster," I said. Again, no response.

I drove him back to his hotel after lunch. Although I had been so hopeful at the start of his visit, by the time we said goodbye, I felt deflated and no closer to finding any clarity.

Yet something compelled me to stay in touch.

# THIRTY-NINE

IN THE SPRING JUST BEFORE my daughter turned ten, my husband's parents invited us to Paris to share an apartment they had rented for a week on Île Saint-Louis.

A lot had changed in the last few years. My son was born, and we moved to Andover, a pretty New England town just twenty-three miles north of Boston. It had quaint white churches, dogwood trees, nearby apple orchards, and was an easy jaunt up to the mountains of New Hampshire and Vermont. We lived in an 1860 high-ceilinged house right on the Main Street campus of the well-known Phillips Academy, Exeter's rival school. I was still commuting thirty minutes regularly into Boston for rehearsals and concerts, and I had founded a chamber music series with my husband that audiences embraced.

Michael couldn't take time off work to accept his parents' offer, so I decided to bring Sophie as a special 10th birthday trip. Michael would stay home with Sasha, our five-year-old son.

"You two are going to have so much fun," my sweet husband said to us in the days before we left.

'You know, Sophie," I jumped in, "every single bistro in Paris is candle-lit and has skinny French fries." *Only there they just call them fries.*

The French windows of our apartment on Quai d'Anjou opened directly onto the banks of the Seine, and we were able to walk easily to many of our destinations. I had never played the tourist when I was a student, but now would have a chance to do so with my daughter—to climb the Eiffel Tower and Sacré Coeur, ride the Bateaux Mouches, and bring her to all my favorite hidden corners of Paris.

Sophie had been my closest confidante since her earliest years. At four, she thoughtfully considered her future and decided, "I want to be a musician like Mommy but I want to be *smart* like Daddy," and consoled me as she looked at the low, horizontal C-section scar I carried from her new baby brother: "It doesn't matter, Mommy; anyway, you *needed* a decoration." She had waved to me in the Boston Ballet orchestra pit from her seat in the front row, and had met an array of famous conductors backstage at Tanglewood during Boston Symphony rehearsals.

I took Sophie's picture as she posed on the steps of the Palais de Justice, with the immense chiseled letters, *LIBERTÉ, EGALITÉ, FRATERNITÉ,* overhead. She looked so small in her short skirt, stubby ponytail, and cross body purse. What did I look like at twenty, I wondered, meeting Luc on these same stairs in 1977?

Each night Sophie and I would venture out for dinner in search of the skinny French fries that I had promised her. We would enter a little restaurant, and as I sipped my large goblet of red wine, Sophie would cozy up with her pad and pencil, and lose herself in drawing ladies with poufy dresses, tiny waists and bouffant hair. I heard her whispering French words that she was starting to recognize: *du pain, du beurre, de l'eau s'il vous plaît, poisson grillé.*

"It's smart that they have pigeon on the menu," my daughter said without looking up from her drawing pad, "'cause there are so many in Paris, they'll never run out."

Luc and I had maintained a spider's silken thread of contact over the last decade. Years would go by and he would scarcely emerge through the deep layers of my past. But then something would trigger a memory—like a French film about a boys' chorus which featured the very song he sang as soloist with *Les Petits Chanteurs*—and I would feel compelled to send him a single line in an email which read, "I just saw *Les Choristes*."

I would later learn that he didn't do email, that his secretary printed out my five-word message, and walked it into his office.

There were several other brief encounters when he came to Boston on business, each one so trivial and unsatisfying that I wondered why I bothered. He had called once when I was pregnant with my son, but after learning this news, suddenly had no time to see me. He questioned me coldly about why I would do such a thing since I already had one child.

After he learned to do email, he would randomly send a brief note after various American tragedies, asking if I was okay. I responded once by saying, "Even in the postmodern era of our history, you had your chance with me." And I didn't mean romantically. I meant that he'd had so many chances to be less emotionally impoverished, so many chances to just try harder to connect. "I'm afraid that ship has sailed," I wrote another time.

But my ambivalence would surface in the form of a phone call from my hospital bed when I lay restless and wretched after undergoing lung surgery, or by including him in a mass email about a concert I was giving at Salle Cortot in Paris. And like an alcoholic in denial who pours liquor down the kitchen sink, I would delete his contact information—phone numbers and email address—and vow never to communicate with him again.

But then I'd find a way.

I told Luc in a letter to his office address that I was coming to Paris with my daughter, and called him once we arrived. Sophie knew this was an old boyfriend of mine, but her understanding of that concept was limited.

"Did you ever kiss Luc?" she asked me as we held hands on the way to his office building in the seventeenth *arrondissement*. She was hopping over cracks in the sidewalk and yanking my hand when I least expected it.

"Not much," I replied, unsure of the protocol when explaining exes to ten-year-olds.

"Mom, do you still have that apple in our bag?" she asked without expecting more. "Who *was* Granny Smith, anyway?"

At 6:30 we arrived at his modern high rise building where we were shown into an imposing top floor suite with immense windows and magnificent views of Paris. Sophie and I were waiting on a cushy leather couch, looking at a large picture book about Brittany on the glass coffee table when Luc walked in.

He smiled self-consciously as we kissed hello, and I introduced him to my daughter. As awkward as all our past encounters had been, Sophie's presence added an additional dimension of inhibition. He asked us about our week. I told him in French that I was failing miserably as a tour guide. (*"Mom, next time can we do Paris countryside?"*)

The three of us rode the elevator down to the underground garage of his office building and got into his car. He put on a CD for my benefit.

"La Musique," he said, with a sweep of his hand.

"Nothing has changed," I said, to please him. It was a beautiful day, so after driving for about ten minutes and finding ourselves on the Left Bank, I asked Luc if we could park near the Jardin du Luxembourg which I hadn't yet shown Sophie. We found a tiny spot on rue Soufflot, and headed toward the tall black iron gates. Sophie and I were swinging our clasped hands as we sauntered past the Medici fountain and the flower beds, and she was bending down to pat all the tiny manicured French dogs. Luc seemed to be rooted in work mode, so I convinced him to take off his jacket and tie and he sullenly obliged.

"I really need to get something to drink," he said, looking desperate to end our stroll after only a short while. We got back in the car, arriving just moments later at the corner of Boulevard du Montparnasse and Boulevard Saint Michel. The neon purple sign of La Closerie des Lilas was directly in front of us now. With a single glance to me as if to get my consent, Luc parked the car nearby. We found a table outside on the terrace in the low sun. It was impossible not to think back to our afternoon English lessons inside the piano bar against the mirrored walls.

"Look at that little dog!" Sophie exclaimed, pointing to a tiny terrier sitting on a chair next to a lady dining alone. "I can't believe they let dogs into restaurants here!" she beamed.

We looked at the menu which I translated for Sophie.

"Mom, will you just order for me?" she asked dismissively, and then added, "Is my book still in your bag?"

I dug through our tote, moving aside my *Plan de Paris,* our two sweaters, umbrella, museum postcards, and drawing pad, and handed Sophie her book, *The Golden Compass,* by Phillip Pullman. She began reading, immersing herself happily in her private world. Luc was visibly affected by her, unable to hide how charmed he was by my little intellectual daughter reading obliviously at the table while he and I spoke in French. He tried to engage her by asking in English what her book was about. She explained it in quick, rambling sentences, and he followed attentively.

"Do you *practeece* every day?" he asked, when he learned she played the piano. He seemed to want to connect with her, to absorb who she was. She nodded yes and smiled and went back to reading. I pulled out a photo of Sasha playing a quarter-size cello, his mouth in an adorable, determined pout, his eyes closed with his long lashes resting against his cheek.

"It's odd, but neither of my children ever showed any interest in music," Luc said wistfully.

I could have predicted that he would have those very thoughts. I knew exactly the effect seeing my musical children would have on him—Sophie, a girl whose face was so much like mine that every person who met her made the same comment: That she was "the portrait of her mother." There was only one thing he could have been thinking: These were the children we might have had together.

When we had finished our quick, unceremonious dinner, Luc said he was very tired, and the conversation seemed to come to an abrupt end. He offered us a ride back to our apartment, and when we arrived, Sophie leaned forward from the back seat of his car.

"Would you like a caramel?" she asked Luc.

"Yes I would, thank you," he answered in English, accepting one that Sophie had taken from her little purse, for perhaps the same reason he had accepted my tea that night in the café decades ago. He then turned to me and said in French, "You see, she's not as shy with me as you thought she'd be."

Luc had originally proposed that we meet again the following night, Friday, in our neighborhood on Île St. Louis, at one of his favorite spots, and I assumed he meant for a longer, more relaxed dinner. Again, I held out hope that maybe this time we might finally succeed in letting down our guard. Luc had also offered to drive us around Paris on Saturday, and Sophie and I were looking forward to having a knowledgeable chauffeur after an exhausting week of taking buses and metros. I imagined a really fun day of sight-seeing and adventures, and the sweet relief of relinquishing my role as tour guide. The arrangement was to call him at his office the next day, Friday, to make a plan for that evening.

Sophie and I said goodbye to him and climbed out of his car on Quai d'Anjou.

"Thanks for dinner. See you tomorrow," I smiled.

Luc had an inscrutable look on his face.

He was not at his office when I called him the next day, nor did he return any of the numerous messages I left with his secretary, on his home phone, or on his cell phone Friday, Saturday, or Sunday, the day Sophie and I left Paris.

As Sophie and I waited in the airport for our flight to take off on Sunday afternoon, we wondered what could have happened to Luc. How was it possible that he had simply vanished? Eating gummy bears and admiring the new jewel tattoos we had adhered to our upper arms, we joked that meeting my beautiful daughter was just too much for him, that he must have had to jump off a Paris bridge after seeing 'what might have been.'

I wondered if I would ever learn the truth.

# FORTY

———— ∞∞∞ ————

"*BONJOUR*, IT'S LUC BERTHELOT," HE said in his typical formal fashion when I answered the phone one afternoon, a few years after I had brought Sophie to Paris. His impromptu calls never failed to knock the wind out of me, but as my heart hammered violently, he told me he was in Boston for a few days and asked if I had any time to meet.

It was odd to me, actually, that Luc felt comfortable enough to call me after all this time—a married woman with two children and a husband who worked from home. It seemed contrary to his modest nature to impose in such a way. Now my whole family was in on the joke about the older French ex-boyfriend who intermittently called out of the blue, the "Luc sweater" still lying around in some closet of old winter clothes. But I tolerated their ridicule, and figured I deserved it, because, against all my better instincts, I wanted to see him again. Yes, it was fun to use my French and play our old conversational games. He brought out a certain feisty and mischievous side of me that stayed dormant with other people. His irrepressible arrogance about so many things made me want to think up clever retorts to put him in his place and when I succeeded, especially in French, I felt victorious. But it was more than that: In spite of all the disappointing past encounters, each time I held out hope that this time might be different. Like Charlie Brown and the football. And I couldn't stop wondering if he, too, wanted to finally say something.

I told Luc that I was playing a semi-staged concert version of *The Magic Flute* at Emmanuel Church that night at 7:30. I could see him after it was over, I said, probably around 10:30 or so. Would that be too late? No problem, he said. He asked if I could come to the Boston Harbor Hotel when I was finished.

I fantasized that Luc would show up at the back of the church and hear me play the ravishing flute solos in the opera, ones that would earn me a solo bow at the end. He had only known me as a student and knew nothing about my career. I remembered a scenario Luc used to invent about the future, decades earlier, when we were still happily together: He described a scene where I was an international soloist and miserably married to a philistine who was only interested in sports and business. Luc would show up secretly at a concert after not seeing me for many years and we would escape out the back door of the green room to run away together. We had laughed and laughed at the lunacy of this story, since at the time it was unimaginable that we would not end up together.

When I hung up, I retrieved his box of old letters from the top shelf of my closet. That box had migrated from closet to closet in five different homes since 1978, and yet there they remained, eerily untouched. I reread some of them for the first time in nearly twenty-five years. The memories of both love and anguish were as real as if our story had happened yesterday. As if I had compartmentalized the pain and preserved it in a deep alcove of my being.

> *Julie, I want to tell you all that you brought me during these months in Paris: your gentleness, your intelligence, and your sensitivity touched me more than you can imagine and tie me to you forever. I cannot conceive of confiding and loving someone if it isn't tied to this notion of the most elevated sense of fidelity . . .*

I sat on the floor, poring over them one at a time, surprised that I still remembered the musical flow of each one so well. There were tears. But I didn't miss Luc. I missed myself at twenty when there was nothing in the world I was more certain that I wanted.

I somehow knew that this would be the last time I saw him.

Luc never made it to my concert, even though I had made a point of mentioning the details to him. When it was over, I changed into jeans, but deliberately kept on a favorite black top I was wearing. I got in my car and headed toward The Boston Harbor Hotel, where new blocks of scaffolding and construction forced me onto streets I didn't recognize. A major snowstorm had been predicted for that evening.

"What am I doing?" I whispered several times under my breath as I turned down incorrect one-way streets, getting farther and farther from the hotel. It felt wrong—that it was late, that I was going out of my way to see him, and that if I hurried home, I might kiss my family good night before they went to sleep. I had long since worked my way back to wholeness and sanity since recovering from this painful love affair. I had landed intact, and, thankfully, in a rich and fulfilled life with a man I adored.

There were evenings when I stood in my kitchen with flour-caked hands trying to perfect my *Tarte Tatin*, a fire burning in the living room, the scent of fall leaves outside. My kids would be playing a piece together in the adjacent music room and asking me to join them. "Mom, come play Haydn Trio with us," they'd say, and my heart would take flight. So why was I here?

When you fall in love at twenty, I wondered, as I drove around lost in the narrow streets of Boston's North End, does the heart form around the other person, like an old tree slowly absorbs a sign hung on it when it was a sapling? And then, when it's gone, do you forever feel the lack of it, feel its imprint, where it once rested?

I called Luc from my flip phone when I could finally see the massive archway of the Boston Harbor Hotel just up Atlantic Avenue. How things had changed since 1977 when there were no cell phones—the endless missed connections, the daily trips to phone booths in café basements! I abandoned my VW Beetle out front with the valet and came hurrying through the lobby just as Luc was coming around the corner from the elevators.

Even though it had only been a few years since I last saw him in Paris with Sophie, I was still surprised to find that he was not the same young man I kept frozen in my memory. He seemed taller than I remembered, and though he was roughly the same weight and still had most of his hair, his face was wider now, and he wore small wire-rimmed glasses. Twenty-five years rendered him a certain type—like a distinguished French-politician now, especially with the white scarf around his neck. His eyes were the pale blue-gray color I remembered. But why had I found him so handsomely debonair when I was young? That attraction was long gone.

"*Julie Scolneek,*" he said with his ever-strong French accent and, with a small self-conscious smile, kissed me on each cheek. There was a sense of irony now, a shared sense of how much time had passed and the immensity of our story.

"Can we find a little restaurant?" he asked. "I know it's quite late, but I just finished my meeting, and I haven't eaten."

The concierge directed us across the street to a small Italian restaurant nearby. We were seated at a corner table and opened our menus. I was tense and my mouth bone dry, so it was hard to imagine consuming anything. I ordered a glass of Pinot Noir without looking at the menu. This seemed to amuse Luc, who glanced at the wine list and ordered a half bottle of a red he recognized. When it arrived, the waiter poured two big goblets. I took a few big gulps which slid down my throat and immediately helped me breath.

Although I had planned on waiting for the right moment, I precipitously reached into my flute bag and took out three CDs and their program booklets. I handed them to him: *Music, Marriage & Madness, In Search of Marcel Proust*, and *Poetic Journeys*. I explained that they were live concert recordings from the chamber music series that I had started a few years back. He read the tracks on the back covers and spent some time flipping through the program booklets.

"*Merci beaucoup,*" he said, seemingly moved by this gift, placing them on top of a thick black spiral notebook he had put next to his plate.

Finally feeling warm, I removed my coat, aware that I was still wearing my favorite black concert top—a stretchy, sleeveless mock turtleneck with cut in shoulders, as well as a gold armlet above my left bicep. This was typical concert dress for me, but I couldn't deny that I had chosen it to look my most alluring. But why? I didn't want Luc. I just wanted him to find me prettier, sexier, and more sophisticated than when he knew me at twenty. But when would I stop wanting him to regret our ending? And when would I stop searching for something more from these visits?

The waiter brought a basket of crusty artisan bread. I tore off a chunk and dunked it in the garlicky olive oil. There were a hundred things that I had hoped we would discuss when I saw him in Paris with Sophie, but we didn't get a chance during that first truncated dinner. Then he had vanished before our second one.

"My daughter sings in a children's chorus," I said a bit too randomly, "and they sang Rameau's *La Nuit* last year."

This was the piece he sang as a boy soprano, the piece that I first heard over the radio in Madame Cammas' apartment, with Luc as the nine-year-old soloist.

"*Ah bon?* Really?" he asked. "I am so surprised that an American children's chorus would know that piece."

"Oh, they didn't," I said. "I told the director about it and found the music for them."

"What has become of Yann?" I asked when it was clear this subject would go no farther. "He must be in his late twenties now?"

"Yes, he's living in London, in graduate school studying economics. My daughter is eighteen. Just finished her *Bac* . . . I'm living with a young woman, well, young for me, an *avocate,* from my law firm. She has two young children."

It never ceased to amuse me that 'lawyer' was the same word in French as 'avocado.'

"*Une avocate?* Really?" I teased him, since we had always made fun of lawyers. I changed my tone. "It must be nice for you to be around little kids again," I said. He nodded.

"What's become of Philippe?" I continued.

"Philippe is divorced from Françoise," he said, "and involved with a very famous woman politician in Paris. He's kind of an idiot; we're not very close, never really were."

"Are you serious? He was your *best* friend!" I teased him in English, laughing, trying to remind him with my tone how many problems we had because of Philippe. He looked embarrassed and protested with a shake of his head.

"You know I have been coming to Paris every fall to give a concert at Salle Cortot," I continued, "and I thought I saw you once, a few years ago. I had just arrived at Place des Ternes, after a rehearsal, and the train was pulling away. I just missed getting on as the doors closed and I think you were on that train. I saw you standing with a newspaper under your arm, in that same olive-green trench coat you always used to wear."

"Yes, it's possible," he said. "My office is very close to Place des Ternes, and I use that metro stop.

Our conversation was like a bad tennis game with no successful rallying, one person serving the ball but never getting a return. Then the second person would serve, and the other would miss again.

"May I take a look at this?" I asked, picking up the big black binder he had placed next to his plate. It was a highly technical legal brief in English.

"You understand this level of English now?" I asked in disbelief as I thumbed through it.

"I *wrote* that *dossier*," he boasted.

It was hard to believe that Luc had mastered the language to such a degree. He was still too self-conscious to speak a word of English in front of me, his former teacher. He had even asked me to order for him in the restaurant.

Our dinners had come and we were eating now. My fish was dry and swallowing was difficult. I took more sips of wine, and was feeling its effect. His pasta and mussels looked much better and he was eating quickly. We ate for a moment in weighty silence.

"Is music still as important to you as it used to be?" I tried again.

"Yes, of course," he answered. "I haven't sung in the chorus for many years but I still go to concerts and to the opera . . . and I listen to my CDs, of course." Another missed serve.

Then I knew it was time to ask.

"Luc, aren't you ever going to tell me what happened in the summer of '78?"

For an instant he looked away with horror, his face twisting in agony, as if he were physically ill. We had never discussed our final scene: his horrible, hurtful behavior in Boston; my leaving him after five days; meeting his wife the night before his return to France; Claire's two letters begging me for information; the inevitable divorce and custody battle. We needed countless hours to crack our vaults of silence and erase the decades that had piled up since then. I suspected he was incapable of discussing it, even now, twenty-five years later. But I needed to talk about it, as if the old grief inside still needed to be released. I didn't want the pain to retreat to its nest for another three decades. I knew this was probably my last chance.

"You know," I continued, even though I was getting nowhere, "I found two letters Claire wrote me back then. She was asking for information about our relationship, for your divorce . . . and custody case."

I knew I was treading on thin ice, but I needed to take the chance. He looked surprised but interested. He asked me what she wrote. I explained as well as I could remember and then I continued.

"I actually did write to her, but the letter never reached her," I confessed.

Indignation sprang from his face. "I cannot believe you would do such a thing," he shot back, shaking his head in disbelief, as if my allegiance to him should have extended beyond our breakup. "I take it you have matured since then," he added.

It was startling how quickly that old familiar venom resurfaced. But finally I was getting a response.

"You deserved it," I almost whispered, looking at him straight in the eye.

His manner relaxed and he tried to coax it back to gentleness. "I would really like to see those letters that she wrote you," he said, when he had finally recovered, "to show my son, to give him a better idea of this time period."

"Are you sure?" I asked. "They don't make you look very good." I couldn't help myself. "She said you tried to use blackmail to prevent the divorce, having been the confidante of her father . . ."

His face had regained its neutral facade after that ever-so-brief letting down of his guard. I saw that it was useless to hope for some kind of explanation. I continued.

"She writes very well, Claire. She tried to use guilt, but assured me that I wouldn't have to appear in court."

"*Moi, I* would have been able to make you appear in court," he said, unable to control the lingering bitterness which welled up from this era.

"That must have been very hard . . . afterwards." I tried to backpedal, assuming that he lost custody of his son.

He nodded imperceptibly, his mouth a tight short line, taking great care to let very little show.

"How often did you get to see Yann?"

"Every other weekend, but the day he turned eighteen, he chose to come live with me. The *day* he turned eighteen!"

"Do you remember when I showed up at a chorus rehearsal, five years after that summer, and I wouldn't get a drink, or even let you drive me back to my hotel? I told you that someone was waiting for me?"

He blinked yes.

"I think I probably traveled three thousand miles just to be able to say that to you."

Nothing registered on his face. Again, an imperceptible nod. He just couldn't.

"Then I came to Paris for a month alone . . . a few years later, and returned to the chorus again. You were standing with Barenboim and deliberately ignored me, no doubt because of how I treated you the first time. There was no way you could have known that this time I was alone and hoping to talk. Do you remember?"

He nodded.

"It took me about ten years to get over you. Then I met my husband."

"And then it was *fini*?"

"*Complètement fini*," I deadpanned.

"I cannot get over hearing you call someone your husband," he continued without warmth. "If you were *my* wife, I wouldn't want you to be having dinner with another man like this."

It may have been hostile, but it was a surprising moment of honesty, and full of subtext. And, of course, he was right. It would have been one thing if our relationship had evolved into a genuine friendship. But it had not. We shared an unresolved history that we were still too static to discuss, and we failed again and again to connect.

But my remarkable husband *did* understand my need to revisit this part of my past. I appreciated and loved him all the more for his tolerance. He was so confident of my love for him that he never felt threatened by my desire to resolve something that lingered persistently from those young years. He considered this delving into my past an integral part of my romantic nature, and after all, as he put it, he was the one who got me in the end.

We sat in silence for a few moments.

"Do you still have my letters?" I asked Luc quietly, not daring to let this chance slip by. But he fell silent behind his glass wall and couldn't answer. His eyes were empty, as if he hadn't heard my question.

"I have yours," I added. *But I needed to be with someone who could inhabit those words and not just write them.*

Maybe I had wanted to hurt him once, and even for many years after our breakup. Maybe I had deliberately made sure that he knew I had beautiful and musical children with a man who was not only just as smart, handsome, and funny, but someone who was infinitely kinder, more compassionate, and selfless. Someone who could deal with Band-Aids. But I wasn't trying to hurt him anymore. No, I yearned for something different now. Gentleness. Wistfulness, maybe. A moment of recognition of what we once had. And I wanted him to say he was sorry. The waiter came and cleared our plates.

I had nearly finished my glass of wine and was feeling more courageous.

"What happened a few years ago when I came to Paris with my daughter? You disappeared," I began, "like a puff of smoke. Did you ever get my phone messages? We wondered if something had happened to you."

He didn't answer right away. And then he spoke.

"People think that they are strong, but they are not," he said, surprising me with such an honest revelation.

"I couldn't in a million years have predicted that I was going to react that way, seeing your daughter," he continued. "She was so sweet, so intelligent, and . . . she looked so much like you, *en plus*. It took me completely by surprise. I didn't go to work the next day, but stayed enclosed in my apartment all throughout the weekend."

"I don't understand," I said.

But I did understand. I understood by the look in his eyes when he asked Sophie gentle questions about her book and when I showed him a photo of my five-year-old son playing the cello. I saw it in his face when I made him laugh with my outspokenness as I did the very first night we met at the chorus.

And perhaps it was the only utterance of regret that I would ever get from Luc.

When we finished at the Italian restaurant, Luc took out his wallet and paid the bill. I still found it disconcerting to see him with an American Express card and trans-Atlantic Blackberry, symbols of success and technology. We walked the few blocks back to his hotel. It had begun to snow a steady blanket of huge lumpy flakes.

"I could make you an espresso in the room," he said.

I didn't answer. We continued to walk back to the hotel in the snow. "Decaf," I answered, a few moments later.

I followed him quietly into the hotel elevator. With any other man this would have meant only one thing. But not Luc.

"My secretary booked me a corner suite; I don't know why," he said sheepishly as we walked down the corridor of his floor. He clicked the door open with his room key, and I followed him in.

I walked around, admiring, with a whisper of mockery, the enormous flat-screen TV, Nespresso machine, and Bose Wave Radio. The king-size bed had been turned down, and two round gold-foiled chocolates placed on the pillow. Luc's formality and ultra-reserve always made me overcompensate and contrive a casualness I didn't actually feel, as if by pretending that we were just two old friends hanging out, it might actually start to feel true. And there was an urgency now to find out how this evening might end, whether it would bring anything into focus.

"May I have one of your chocolates?" I asked him.

"Of course, take them both," he said. I slipped one into the pocket of my pea coat, keeping one in my hand.

He dropped a red decaf capsule into the Nespresso machine, and pushed a button that forced frothy espresso to trickle instantly into a tiny white cup. The aroma was intense.

*"Tiens,"* he said as he handed it to me.

*"Merci."* I sat down on the edge of the bed and sipped it. Even through my jeans the bed linens felt luxurious. I searched for the local classical music station on the Bose radio. When I found it, I put down my espresso cup and let my torso drop down to the bed, feet still on the floor. Tipsy from the wine, I stayed like that for a moment while I unwrapped one of the chocolates. *Good—milk, not dark.*

Luc took off his coat and lay down on the other side of the bed. After a few moments, I wiggled out of my pea coat and swung my legs up and around with one gentle motion so that I was lying on my back, too. We both lay staring upward at the ceiling, three feet apart on the king size bed, listening to the radio. It took us back almost twenty-five years to a time when listening to music together was our most cherished shared pastime.

"The piano is too loud," he said.

"Still the expert," I answered.

A few minutes later, I started to get up to leave, but something made me shift onto my side, facing him. I inched over and brought my head lightly to the nook of his chest and shoulder. I am not sure why I did this, but most likely it was a last-ditch effort to connect in any way I could. I was curious to see if it might feel familiar, actually, after lying in this position with my husband hundreds, probably thousands of times during the past fifteen years. Does one man's shoulder feel like another? His arm came around me tentatively and rested on the small of my back. We lay there motionless, except for the small caresses of his fingers on the bare skin of my waist between my jeans and the bottom edge of my black top. The snow was coming down harder outside.

"I should leave," I said, not moving.

"Five more minutes," he whispered.

A few minutes later, I got up quietly. Luc watched me put on my coat and scarf and then stood up, too.

"Are you going to be okay . . . driving home in the snow?" he asked.

I smiled softly and nodded. And then I faced him.

"You know, Luc," I said, "it really *was* a good thing we never got married."

His lips pursed a tiny smile and he blinked that he understood. I wondered if he actually knew what I meant, since I wasn't completely sure myself. That, even if I hadn't discovered his true colors that summer, it would never have lasted; that we would have made each other miserable; that sharing poetry and music didn't create happiness, but making a life with a man whose every small and large gesture incarnated love in the present, physical world, did.

"But probably all you had to say to me was, 'I cannot live in the United States. I need you to live in Paris with me.'"

It was astonishing how the old wound opened up again, and how, for the briefest instant, I had forgotten how perfectly my life had turned out. How, at the central crossroads of my life, I had known the right decision to make.

"*C'est pas mal comme histoire.* It's not a bad story," Luc almost whispered.

"Goodbye, Luc," I said, feeling certain that this night was our last shot and that we would never have another. We embraced tentatively, and I lingered a moment, resting my cheek against his chest. With one final look at his pale blue eyes, I walked to the door, opened it, and heard it close heavily behind me. I imagined a Hollywood movie scene in which he would call my name and not let me walk through the door.

"*Julie*," he would say, in his French accent, and I would stop in my tracks without turning around. The soundtrack would swell as I'd pivot and fall back into his arms. But he didn't call my name, and I left without turning for a final glance. Those I loved far more than memories were waiting for me at home. I felt calm as I rode the elevator down to the lobby and got into my car in front of the hotel. At peace. The story was finally over. After twenty-five years, I could finally close the book. I needed to feel Luc's love again to release the grief that had been hermetically sealed away in an unspoken corner of my heart. This was as close as I would get.

I didn't find the answers I was looking for that night, but as I drove north on the highway, thick, clumpy flakes slanting down hypnotically onto my windshield, something came to me: Luc's vision of the world—the one of music, poetry, and imagination, the one he shared so well with me in Paris and through his letters—was beautiful and rare, but it was only one color. Blue. The only color he could literally see. The blue of Picasso and other artists who used the single hue to create a mood of melancholy, emptiness, and isolation—all of the elements which dominated Luc's life.

Maybe Luc's colorblindness wasn't his inability to see reds and greens after all, but his limited vision of the world. Perhaps it was my own blindness that prevented me from seeing who Luc was then and who he could never be for me. Part of the wistful ambiguity of recalling that time through the long lens of my subsequent life was understanding who I had not yet become.

But the imagery would last a lifetime, and fragments from those young Paris vignettes still flowed like light through the prism of my days. I thought of the lines from "Tintern Abbey," the Wordsworth poem I tried to teach Luc under the eaves on rue Bonaparte. They rang truer than ever:

> The picture of the mind revives again:
> While here I stand, not only with the sense
> Of present pleasure, but with pleasing thoughts
> That in this moment there is life and food for future years.

The words of the poem had not changed, but now, heading home in the dark under a falling canopy of snow, I understood them in a way that I couldn't then. What did I know at twenty about memories that could endure for decades? Wordsworth reminded me that our pasts are not to be mourned, but treasured, and that what I had left of myself and Luc on rue Bonaparte in 1977 enriched me daily with *"life and food for future years."*

The beauty and sadness of that certain shade of blue and of that little boy soprano from my dreams still dwelt within me, even as I drove home in the night towards the beautiful life I had built with my present loves, here and now.

# EPILOGUE

———◦⊱⊰◦———

IT WAS PAST MIDNIGHT WHEN I got back to my house, now dark and quiet, with my family asleep inside. I put down my flute bag by the front door, savoring for a moment the quiet warmth of a happy home. Slinging my pea coat over the banister, I started up the stairs, but stopped half-way up to look at the framed photos of my children on the wall. Each was a moment plucked from our family history—Sophie and Sasha playing together in piles of crunchy, fall leaves; Sasha tangled up impishly in a dozen red helium balloons; Sophie at six with a coquettish smile in a Little Bo Peep costume, clutching her two-year-old brother, a cotton-ball-covered little sheep, to her chest.

I crept into Sophie's room to kiss her good night.

"Love you," my daughter murmured from deep within her reveries, always sensing when I needed to hear it most. In Sasha's room I tripped over his fencing mask before leaning over his bed to straighten out his east-west position and kiss his moist, matted hair in the darkness. A rush of love washed over me when I entered my own bedroom and saw Michael asleep on his side. Inhaling his warm sleep scent, I leaned in to kiss his cheekbone and cover his cool, bare shoulder with the duvet.

"Are you coming to bed?" he said without opening his eyes. "How was the opera?" I always appreciated what a light sleeper he was. And then, teasing me gently, even from semi-consciousness, "How was *Luc?*"

"Shhh. Don't wake up. I'm going downstairs for a while," I whispered. I undressed in the dark as our Rubenesque calico cat, Anya, rubbed up against my bare calves, and took a little love nibble. After slipping on Michael's flannel pajama bottoms and sweatshirt, both balled up on the floor, I walked downstairs with my laptop under my arm. I looked through the mail on the console by the front door and went into the kitchen to put the tea kettle on. Bringing my mug of tea into the living room, I turned on a dim lamp, slid open the CD bins, and ran my finger absently along the B's: Bach, Beethoven, Berlioz, Brahms. I slipped Beethoven's String Quartet, Op. 130, into the CD player, and skipped to the *Cavatina*[15] movement, keeping the volume low.

I was settling into a deep, chenille love seat with my laptop when Anya hoisted her ample weight into the space next to me, emitting a low rumbling purr the moment her claws dug into my flanneled thigh. And then I remembered: There was one more chocolate from Luc's hotel room in the pocket of my coat. I went to retrieve it and settled down again, Anya reclaiming her spot at my side. Unwrapping the gold foil, I dunked the round disk into my tea and licked off the melted layer of chocolate.

When I said goodbye to Luc that night, I couldn't stop thinking about a chilling short opera by Gian Carlo Menotti called *The Medium,* another record that my mother introduced to us when my sisters and I were young, haunting though it was for children. In the story, a mute servant boy, Toby, lives with a deceitful medium and her beautiful daughter, Monica, with whom he is deeply, and not so secretly, in love. As he cannot speak for himself, Monica goes behind him in their make-believe games, and sings as if she is *his* voice, in a heart-rending love song to herself: "*Monica, Monica, can't you see, that my heart is bleeding, bleeding for you?*"[16]

Luc was no less impaired than Toby, I thought, as I stroked my silky companion nestled at my hip. He may not have been physically mute, but he lived a considerable portion of his life detached from the rest of the world, imprisoned by his inability to connect. For decades I had tried hopelessly to have a deeper, sweeter exchange with him about our past, a wistful moment of looking back, to feel his affection once again, hear his regret, and find the closure I needed. But it never happened. Like Monica assuming Toby's voice, I tried to imagine the letter he might write me, if only he could, that would finally melt away my long-buried grief. I opened my laptop, and began typing:

*Dear Julie,*

*It has taken me several years to be able to put into words the effect that seeing you again has had on me. Beyond my usual difficulty in communicating, I am even more paralyzed now because you belong to someone else. Your beautiful family and current life speak volumes of your past and future without me.*

*When we saw each other for those few moments at the chorus, just five years after our ending in Boston, it already felt as if no time had passed at all. But seeing you again recently, after twenty-five years? It is evidence of such timelessness that it is scarcely believable. That you are still able to bring me to this place of comfort and trust in your presence, is unfathomable to me. But I cannot play and laugh as you can so easily, knowing that your family is waiting for you at home. I must stay guarded.*

*You asked about music in my life. If you only knew the irony! It is still my single greatest love in this world and yet it also torments me daily. Every note I hear reminds me of how I lost my chance at happiness with the only woman who ever shared it deeply with me. When the sound of a flute emerges suddenly through my car radio, it is a knife in my heart, a mocking reminder of how I alone am responsible for the life I chose.*

*All those years ago when I was afraid of losing my son in a divorce, I made you suffer waiting for me to be free. I lost custody of Yann, anyway, and I lost you, too. Why didn't I run after you, when*